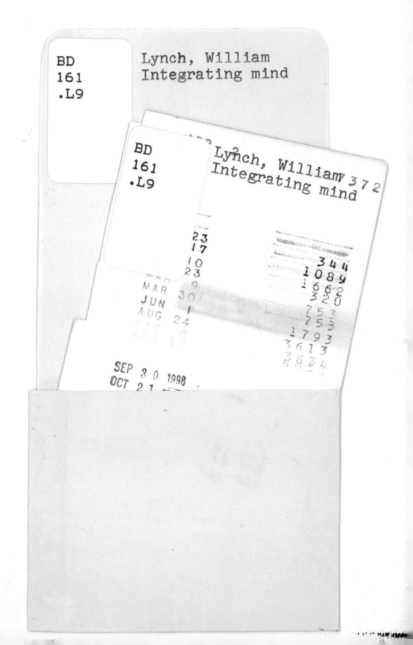

The Integrating Mind

An Exploration Into Western Thought
WILLIAM F. LYNCH, S.J.

SHEED AND WARD · NEW YORK

PREFACE

I had a professor once whose typical summary of a book would be: "The author gives it away on page 289." A writer hates to summarize or give away a book in a sentence or two, but the fact is that this is a book written in defense of a way of thinking and a philosophy of life that may be called both-and versus either-or. Put negatively, it is an attack on all unnecessary alternatives and unnecessary conflicts, especially in our national society. Put more philosophically, it is a defense of contrariety, that is, of the constantly recurring fact that many contraries, instead of constituting alternatives for choice, are mutually creative of each other and cannot live without each other.

It has been one of the great and pre-eminent tasks of the civilized mind of the West to find this out and to develop the discovery in the concrete. It takes time, it takes culture and history, to keep refusing the easy way and the easy passion, to keep working at the reconciliation of mind and body, subject and object, person and society, freedom and law, the obsolescent and the historical, the theological and the human reality, and many other things. This task is itself a passion, but not an easy one, nor a venture into the middle of the road. It has been the vocation of the civilized mind, the mind of the West.

It leaves us at only an apparent disadvantage against our great enemies of today. Only on the surface do they have the advantage, seeming like giants, able to wheel around in infinite space with complete freedom of decision, thought and feeling, opting for absolute and total forms of thought and action, while we in the West must put more things together and keep more things together. But these simplicities hide terrible weaknesses. The totally dependent man is terribly weak; the totally independent man is terribly weak; but not he who with integrated passion puts the two together. Indeed we badly need a common national purpose, but let it not be a shibboleth or a gimmick. Let it be, in hundreds of forms, the restoration of the total and difficult idea of man and the human. For of what use is courage and of what use is passion if it is not willing to get down to the difficult detail and contrariety of the human?

Charles de Gaulle has said that Russia belongs to the West and must return to it. About that I do not know. Only God does, although we can hope, without being naive. But for ourselves, we can do more, since we can actually *choose* to return to the ideas of the West. I do not believe, as Mr. Belloc was often accused of believing, that the West is the sum total of civilization, but its history does represent an enormous part of civilization. This book investigates one central facet of that history: the meaning and value of the idea of contrariety.

ACKNOWLEDGMENTS

The author gratefully acknowledges the kindness of the editors of *Thought, Cross Currents* and *The Critic,* the directors of the Fund for the Republic, and the President and Trustees of the College of New Rochelle, for permission to use here material which first appeared in their pages or which was first developed at their request. A particular debt of gratitude is owed to University Publishers, Inc. for their kind permission to reprint, in a substantial though abridged form, excerpts from my study, *An Approach to the Metaphysics of Plato Through the Parmenides.*

CONTENTS

CONTENTS

THE INTEGRATING MIND

An Exploration Into Western Thought

1

THE TOTALISTIC TEMPTATION

This book is in substance a plea that we keep things together that belong together. We could sum that substance up in a number of ways.

It is first and foremost a many-phase analysis of the disease of the clear or pure idea, in the many forms of that disease that reign among us in our contemporary national culture. I like to call it the univocal idea, born of the univocal intelligence, insisting as it does on a kind of absolute unity of thought or feeling and forbidding any muddying of the waters by the introduction of anything so crass or confusing as reality. Such thinking and thinkers can be magnificent in purity and strength; they can put us lesser mortals to shame, until we become aware that here there is really no thinking going on at all, and that magnificence is being used as a defense against the absence of thought.

Who does not long at times with all his heart for the perfectly clear idea or situation? It would make all our decisions easier; it would simplify the whole of life; it would take all the pain and frustration out of it. Such difficult things as adjustment of the idea to the next moment of history or its integration into other demanding ideas would no longer be necessary. We could thus eliminate all movement and effort. Indeed we should not have to get out of bed in the morning. For we would have arrived at *the* idea or *the* situation that would take care of everything. Like the thoughts of a child, such an idea and mode of life is passive and omnipotent. The child wants what he wants; he has an overriding idea; he does not yet know that other people and other ideas exist. His first tastes of the latter do not produce adjustment or integration, but confusion, fury and another omnipotent proposition.

Such thinking has a deceptive strength and clarity about it. On the surface it is passionate and brilliant over against all lesser comers. In order to keep its position, which it always must at any cost, it must *take over,* rule the roost and not countenance any opposition. It is therefore always a bit of a bully. And it has a cleverness all its own which mimics the saints. Knowing very well that there are indeed such things as choices, commitments and a whole area of either-or in this life, it counterfeits this part of our necessary spirituality before God and man, trumpeting out its virtue, warning against all compromise and double-dealing, averring that it, for one, will never be guilty of such base things.

Of course, we have to get to know the difference between the real thing and the false in such matters. There is need for focus, passion and energy in life. Life is impossible without some approximation to them. Baudelaire said that especially as a man get older, he must learn to concentrate his forces and not be adjusting to every wind. Kierkegaard spent much of his life berating the "aesthetic man," who had no single center but became everything he touched, in complete diffusion of himself. Today we are preoccupied with the problem of, the need of, the search for, the identity of our souls, and we all fear the diffusion of this best of all possessions. We are alarmed over this problem of identity, and there can be no greater source of concern for human beings. Therefore we are today especially open and vulnerable to anything that sharply resembles the discovery at last of a real goal, a real definition for all our energies, real reasons for living, as supports for and creators of our very existence and identity. To the degree that this is true we are open to the influence of the pure idea and all its deceptions.

The fact that we exist in such a relative vacuum is no reason to jump at filling it too quickly. It is hard to endure a vacuum, but sometimes the temporary enduring is better than filling it with the wrong thing. After all, this is nothing other than the virtue we call *waiting*, where that is necessary, and it is a first cousin to hope. Waiting, hope, the plodding, varying workings out of a commitment, decision or insight, require as much passion and strength as their more distant cousin, the univocal intelligence, but it is simply a different passion and a different strength. So it would be wise if those who choose, but also choose against the dangerous purity of the clear idea, would not allow themselves to be trapped into the gambit of choosing between the too limited choices of non-feeling, conservatism, and insensitivity over against the apparent magnificence of the single, absolute idea.

I

These are some of terms of the discussion into which I enter in the following chapters. But these remarks do not at all point to the basic terms of the debate. They are pertinent, very pertinent, but if left to themselves the chances are that they would only add to the hostility in the air between the two camps. They would get stuck in the status of personal charges of one psychology or characterology against another. No, *the terms of the discussion most certainly revolve rather about the innermost structure of reality.* If this is so, as I think it is, then we can begin to look for those impersonal grounds out of which personal agreements between opposed groups might very well develop. Any other way may be interesting, but also surely endless.

What we need is an epistemology, a way of thinking, and a corresponding set of helps for the human passions that will match the structure of reality itself. In a sense, the search into this structure is, of course, endless. Nevertheless, there have been some basic and continuing forms of search which have stood the test of time and have proved fruitful. One of them has been the long-term examinations, by the Western mind, of *the deep interpenetrating relationship of the contraries.* As all of the chapters to come are investigations of the relationship in the concrete between some set of contraries in our national culture, I would like to indicate how I for one became interested in the metaphysical problem of contrariety and how it came increasingly to appear as one medication for the mistake of the pure idea, for all the ideologies and voluntarisms that spring from that particular monster. I am sure that it was a period of early studies of this technical problem in philosophy that did much to create the habit of keeping together in an interlocking group things that belonged together. Of course we deceive ourselves if we do not recognize that there are other things than academic studies that do this for us: life itself, common sense, good friends and teachers. But taking these precious things for granted, there *is* such a critically important thing in the lives of all of us as the intellectual history of the race, and we are fools if we do not profit by it.

It is the custom among us, not without a good deal of

reason behind it, to take Descartes as the whipping boy, since he, at a critical time in the history of the West, drove us decisively in the direction of the pure and univocal idea and away from the great human art of the interpenetration of the contraries. Certainly he solidified, if he did not create, a dangerously absolute distinction between the subject and the object, from which we are now trying desperately to recover. And his fundamental *method*, which was quickly lifted, if not by himself then by all the lesser Cartesians, onto the philosophical plane, depended altogether on the clear idea, that is, on the kind of idea that could in its perfect boundaries be blocked off perfectly from every other idea. As much as anything else we can put our fingers on, the Cartesian method states the position of an absolute distinction between all ideas, of interpreting everything as an either-or. We shall return to this point in Chapter Three.

There is, however, little sense in getting bogged down here in the effort to determine principal villains. It is far more important to understand that this debate between purity and interpenetration is a perennial human debate. My own awareness of this came from fortunate years of study of Greek philosophy.

It became clear to me that even so early Plato had been handed his own unique version of the problem of the clear and dominating idea with its own denial of interpenetration. Every schoolboy in philosophy knows Parmenides had declared that being altogether and totally *is,* and that nonbeing altogether and totally *is not,* and that never the twain shall meet or interpenetrate each other. But what the schoolboy is not quite aware of is the inevitable manner in which this apparently technical and trivial dichotomy spreads out, first of all into a similar war between other contraries and finally into a multitude of actual and concrete problems, some of which we try to tackle in this book.

It makes me think more and more that the only finally
effective way to teach philosophy to the young or the old is
in such a way that the center and the circumference of our
studies come together in a constantly interlocking and mutually illuminating way. Thus, there could be a careful study,
at the center, of whatever issue in metaphysics is under in-
spection, at the same time that there is a concrete investigation of the issue as it reverberates, on the circumference,
in history, literature, sociology, science or whatever actual
fields are involved. Perhaps it would be even better to reverse this order and to come at the formal problem in philosophy only when we have some heuristic reason to think
that it really is a human problem. At any rate I think there
is a real need of keeping this center and this circumference
in constant touch with each other. Else we will pay the price
of a nominalistic and verbal study of philosophy, a bright
game for the young and a trade for the old.

Plato set up for us some of the correct and central pro-
cedures of human thought and some of the fundamental
guides to the structure of reality. Like any philosopher, he
was looking for unity but he did not allow this passion for
unity to push him into too hasty a drive from the many to
the one. His supreme achievement was to modify, control
and discipline the severe rigidity of the Parmenidean divisions between absolute dichotomies. In his own dialogue,
the *Parmenides,* which Hegel called the finest masterpiece
of Greek philosophy, his powerful mind wove all the great
contraries together, so that they were there but inseparably
there, creating each other, depending on each other: the
one and the many, being and non-being, like and unlike,
motion and rest, the great and the small, the equal and the
unequal, and so on. When he finished this metaphysical task,
non-being was no longer on the outside of being, the many

no longer outside the one. He had made thinking that much more difficult, but he had made it truer.

Those who know the extremely difficult nature of the *Parmenides* will forgive a writer when he says that he spent a substantial part of fifteen years trying to unravel that document and to study its method of thinking things out. Looking at these essays and this attempt at a concretion of the same method, I see now that the experience left an indelible mark on me. We keep talking in our academic way of the great experiences of the human race at those moments which we call the Hebraic and the Greek, but for Plato to recreate the Greek moment, apparently devoid of help and facing the human fact, the mixed-up contrariety of the whole business, with such competence, does really tantalize us out of all understanding. Greatness with straightness does not emerge so often.

To become biographical can mean, not the personal, but that one suddenly realizes one's dependence on the march of the mind of the West. Descartes is only an interlude, Plato, very great, only a beginning. To be ensconced in this march is to recognize not a great presence, that terrible existential word, but the movement of a growing achievement that defies absolute unity and absolute totalism, and tries to think, in human terms, in the presence of God. This march is working at unity as much as is any form of totalism or pure idea, but it is doing it with the instruments of the interpenetration and integration of all the forces in and outside of us that are involved. In the case of Plato the principle document for the study of the interpenetrating contraries was the *Parmenides;* the outstanding document that analyzes the integrating process had been the *Republic.*

I am not trying to deify Plato. I am simply giving one man's version of how and where he thinks he made his first important contacts with the mind of the West. That mind

keeps expanding. It has had many heroes. But it also keeps
contracting and periodically threatens to be overcome by the
very demons it is perpetually trying to master, the ideologist,
the totalist, the man of the absolutely clear idea. We are in
such a stage of human history right now, when the demons
are unusually strong and, on the surface, magnificent. We
are disturbed and anxious because we are engaged in an
attempt to master and match these forces without creating
their equivalents in ourselves. We do not yet have the way
or the confidence and seem to be threatened by vacuums
and the lack of purpose. "Seem" is a weak word. The West *is*
threatened. And the temptations are very great, the temptations to many of the forms of totalism.

I have borrowed this word totalism from the vocabulary,
and the context in which it is used, of a recent book which
I have admired very much for its competence and insights:
*Thought Reform and the Psychology of Totalism, A Study
of "Brainwashing" in China,* by Robert Jay Lifton. It is a
book that should be very valuable in communicating an
understanding of the scientific psychological tactics of Communism, and is born out of the new theoretical work of
Erik Erikson on the problems of personal identity and ideology. The author describes it as "a psychological study of
extremism and totalism—and even more broadly, a study
of the 'closed' versus the 'open' approaches to human
change." It is a thoroughly detailed and thoughtful study
of a process which breaks down into two carefully structured steps: 1) The new psychic manipulator makes it his
first business to locate and concentrate on the "negative
identity" of the victim, i.e., on the part of our self-image
which in fact or fantasy falls short of or violates the positive
image, the soul, the ideal. This scientific and destructive concentration aims at causing the negative identity to be seen

as a totalism and totally guilty, incapable of producing anything out of its own inner resources as counteragent and cure. The victim "begins to experience one of the most primitive and painful emotions known to man, the fear of total annihilation." 2) The victim is now ready to surrender himself to an external and all-powerful force, the source of rebirth, of all good, and of the restoration of existence itself. His identity is reshaped entirely in terms of this new and perfect life.

The one totalism, of evil, makes the other, of "good," possible. Extreme is cured by extreme, pure idea by pure idea. One would have to put the psychological analyses of such a book as Dr. Lifton's together with such an historical analysis of the eschatological invasions of the absolute into the political life of the modern world as has been made by Eric Voegelin to understand even better the terrible habit of the polarization of extremes that lies about us in many forms. In this particular discussion (and how clear it is to our enemies) we may be quite certain that the growing Manichaean sense among us, the excessive sense of evil in our nature and in things outside of us, breeds guilt, but it is the kind of guilt that leads to submission. Nor is it ever a submission to God or the truth, but to anything. It becomes a disease of submission to anything.

What happens here of course is that the normal interpenetration of imperfection and perfection in things human and finite gets perfectly sorted out and polarized, each becoming an absolute. And the pain of the apparent absolute in evil is so altogether intolerable to the spirit of man, that it must submit, for very relief's sake, to that absolute good which comes to stand in the place of God. This is the most ancient trick of all, that we who are deluded into thinking of ourselves as absolutely evil should be lead into the coun-

terfeit of that which is absolutely good. The Spirit of evil
appears in the form of the good. It is a trick we play on
each other when we seek to dominate, but when kingdoms
play at the game, then the trouble is immense. It is no
wonder then that the saints have written careful treatises,
carved out of suffering, warning us against the tactics of the
evil which appears in the spirit of light.

This kind of potential submission, ready for further polarization, is alive in the West, thinking it is not good enough
for goodness and decision, preoccupied with its own guilt,
ready, like a child, at the one pole, to submit to the new
saint, the illustrious, dominant saint at the other pole. I do
not think it will work, but all I am saying is that this is the
process. At this moment we can hardly think of an action of
ours that would not be declared invalid by our enemies.
The brainwashing, based on such a polarizing of the contraries, is in process. Our sins are so great, so enormous; let
us meditate upon them, not in degree, but night and day.
There has never been such guilt. Let there be an appro-
priate rolling of drums. Let us then submit, as though at
long last, like bad children who have learned their lesson,
we were ready for our pole, our dunce cap in the corner,
before a new father who knows best.

Thus the metaphysical question, of contrariety or the lack
of it, apparently so harmless, comes out of hiding and emerges
into the forefront of our lives. It does not matter whether
the new hero is from the far right or the far left. The idea
is clear. He knows best and we know nothing. These are
the terms. They are not the terms of all those earthly fathers
whom we love, all those men who use authority with humility and who finally pass on even their ability to a new
generation, to children to whom, rather than destroying,
they have communicated a deeply internal self-respect and
the internal freedom of their own souls.

II

Even here, perhaps here above all, there is room and need for some fascinating studies on the interpenetrating relationship between authority and freedom. Much work remains to be done on this question. I only make a few remarks about it here.

Our usual understanding of the relationship between authority and freedom is that the one is external to the other. Authority is thought of as a policeman or disciplinarian who sees to it that freedom does not overstep its bounds or become itself. There is mutual fault in this relationship, so conceived, and it is the goal of the New Testament to overcome the mutual fault. Authority can be afraid of freedom. Freedom is afraid of itself and therefore flies to authority as a means of not becoming itself, as a medication for that anxiety which freedom causes. What authority should rather do is to communicate and create freedom. Where it forbids, it should forbid souls not to be free. Authority should be zealous to communicate itself to the interior of other people. Freedom, on the other hand, is so frightened at itself that it needs authority to sanction itself. It needs to know that it is all right to be free, and that autonomy has no necessary connection whatsoever with hostility. I begin to think that it is impossible for freedom to do this by itself.

Perhaps it must be communicated by others, by one person to another, a mutual gift. St. John tells us that we are gods. By this I think he means that God, who is absolutely autonomous and inwardly self-ruling, has communicated an inward participation in this autonomy and self-rule to us. Autonomy is not only all right, it is commanded. It is the critical point in us where we imitate God most deeply. Thus the theological movement of the soul toward God and the anthropological movement of the soul toward its own precious autonomy become one and the same act and moment, interpenetrating and without opposition.

Thus what we are finally talking about is nothing but love itself. A neurotic relationship is not love, because the partners are concerned that each should not be free. It is frustrating and self-defeating because it aims at closeness and by its methods prevents or destroys it. Love communicates freedom and by this separation the parties come closer together.

The life of the Trinity is the final and ultimate ground for such a metaphysics. There is a mutual and total communication of self to the other by the Father, the Son and the Holy Spirit. What is given is one and the same nature, so that there is but one God. The communication, however, is not destructive but creative. The counterpart of this communicated common nature is the rebounding of the Persons into absolute autonomy. We have some human hint of this mystery in this sentence: he who loses himself shall find himself.

The function of authority, then, is to create freedom. It must not use men for its own needs but must help men to stand on their own feet. This it will find very hard to do, but all that we expect of it is that it keep trying, keep working at the task. As for freedom, it will be a shock to it to be told that it is a gift, to be received from the outside.

In fact, this is the most difficult of all our interpenetrating contrarieties: to think that autonomy must come from authority, the inside come from an outside. Any form of passivity or receiving seems hard for American culture to handle. But for our last consolation let us remember that it is necessary on the part of those who receive *that they take*. There are those who will take and those who will not take freedom, just as there are those who will give and will not give.

The art of happiness has many definitions. One of them

would be that the givers and the takers of freedom find each other out and live with each other. The finding and the living will help them help everybody else.

Where there is a final refusal of this interpenetration we have the only either-or that really matters. It will be the division between those who love and those who have irreconcilably chosen hate. So many, so varied and so hidden are the forms of love that we can hope that few really choose the second. It is a final mystery, this either-or, this mystery of iniquity, which only God can judge. It would be better if we left that last of all matters to Him. The judgment involves a book no man will ever write.

As for all other intermediate either-ors, I simply have not discussed them in this book. Indeed one must choose in life, and that would be another subject. But even had we chosen this other subject, that of either-or, even then we could not have thereby eliminated the need of a metaphysics of both-and. Decision and the pure idea are not in any sense equivalents, although, as we have seen, the latter in its weakness loves to masquerade under the strength of the former. Even when we decide and choose, reality does not exonerate us from the conditions of humanity and the finite. One of the first conditions of either, no matter what we choose, is that of what we have been calling the mutual interpenetration and intercreativity of the contraries.

What I have done is to select a representative number of concrete problems and situations which stand at the circumference of that central point of the circle we have thought of as the metaphysical point of contrariety. Or we can say that that point breaks out like a prism into the many facets of human life, politics, culture. It takes many analogical forms, but it is always there. I do not call it confusion or ambiguity, because it seems to me to be more structured in its ontology than these contemporary phrases would imply.

"Confusion," as ordinarily used, means a lack of clarity, as though the clarity implied would be a virtue if we had it. As the scholastics used the word "confused," something positive was meant, a universal, intercreative and inseparable fusion of principles. This was the philosophical mode which helped them to handle such relations as those between thought and the object, the same and the different, being and non-being. They had no regrets about the lack of "clarity" that emerged from this central dialectic. Such clarity is a pure myth, and does more harm than good when we try to think within its terms on any area of the real order of things.

These essays, then, are based on no such clarity. One other remark is very much in place. There is a difference between locating the philosophical issue of the structure of reality— the present chapter has tried that briefly—and locating the concrete facets of the issue in our civilization, as the remaining chapters try to do. The latter requires the continuous exercise of judgment, intuition, common sense. Therefore it is more fallible and requires the work of many minds. Indeed it is the task of the whole of human civilization and history to work it out. These essays take their circumscribed place within that long effort. No doubt they are very fallible, in handling such delicate puttings-together. No doubt that, as with the most of men, they occasionally pick a both-and where an either-or is called for. I should just hope that even if this is so it should not be allowed to obscure the validity of the general method. I would hope that the reader, rather than throw out the baby with the bath, would supply his own corrections and insights, and go on himself with the work of synthesis which we all have to do.

1. The first of these successive studies deals largely with the increasing failure of America to contact its own history and the serious consequences of this failure in terms of

anxiety and a moralistic over-extension of the either-or way of thinking into vast areas of human life.

2. The chapter "Divided We Stand" proposes that those on the political far right and far left are both victims of a process of polarization that is rooted in the philosophy of the clear idea.

3. "The Problem of Freedom" is an analysis of one of the abiding points of discussion in Western philosophy: the deep, interpenetrating and creative relationship between freedom, a kind of infinite, and the finite, a form of law or necessity.

4. "Culture and Belief" raises the epistemological question of whether the human mind can think straight if it does not think within some kind of community. It looks at the relation between individual and community.

5. "Toward a Theatre of Public Action" is an examination of the concentration of much of our art on the private. It looks at the collapse of the contrariety *private-public.*

6. It is more difficult to summarize what I try to do in the chapter on "Theology and Human Sensibility." I tackle a frequent misconception of both theology and art as "transcendental," in various pejorative senses of that word, to the human experience and reality. The chapter is, therefore, an attempt to bring the "transcendental" and the finite into a closer, interpenetrating relation.

Finally, I have added a short supplement of chosen passages from my own philosophical analysis of the problem of contrariety in Plato as it appeared in *An Approach to the Metaphysics of Plato Through the Parmenides.* So much work has to be done, in our new terms, on this philosophical question, that I do this as a reminder of the complexities of the issue. It may also help to pull the two parts of the book, speculative and concrete, closer together.

2

THE AMERICAN ADAM

Let us begin with a general glance at the American situation. If man, as I shall suggest, is a tactile creature who suffers to the degree that he is not in touch with the reality of himself and things and others, then it is proper to raise the question of the consequences for the American Character when it is not in adequate touch with its own history and the general history of man. I deal therefore with the complex, in that character, of what we can call the American Adam, or the man who has no past and is intent on being a new and absolute beginning in history. This part of our character has certainly had its noble, creative and liberating side, but I deal with it as it has become autonomous, free-wheeling, out of hand, exaggerated and exaggerating. A very special question I will raise about it is whether it does not tend to create a painfully moralistic rather than a moral civilization, whether, correspondingly, it does not tend ironically, over against its original intention, to take away the true liberty of the children of God.

Before we get to that point I am going to propose, as a substrate and an introduction, that there is indeed and must be a consensus among us as to the nature of the American Character, but that unfortunately this consensus is double. One consensus is historical, actual, free and interior, a real meeting of minds about our identity. The other is a-historical, anonymous, neither free nor interior, coming from the outside of us or felt as an invader when it is on the inside. It is an agreement that is agreed to by nobody. It is created by a vacuum, by the vacuum of the absence of the historical.

The interaction of these two forms of consensus as to the identity of the American Character is fascinating and must be carefully studied. The failure to determine and preserve the one, the historical, will provide the perfect breeding ground for the other, the a-historical, the enslaving, the anonymous. Actually our air is alive today with the concern for this distinction. In the academic world we are uneasy with the definition of education as a way of adjusting to each other and wish to re-establish the historical disciplines, so that we may know something and be what we know and are, letting adjustment take care of itself as a more secondary process. In public affairs we are searching for a public purpose, for we know very well that the more we lack purpose the more we are preoccupied with national prestige and the need of finding out, no matter what we are, what people think we are. In a word, Freud and Harry Stack Sullivan must be writhing in their graves at the emphasis on interpersonal relations between people who are not yet persons. This is a consensus between those who are not free and it is one of the great sources of moralism.

We must distinguish, therefore, between two parts of our culture and between two definitions of the American Character. Whatever it is in detail, the first is the real American Character, and has its foundations in real history; it has survived the tests of history; it exists at the interior of us, in

the true sense of the word *interior*, not only as something
that we are but also wish to be; it is not only acceptable to
the individual but it makes other people acceptable to us
and vice versa; it is therefore a true consensus, the kind of
consensus which forms a real community, a real meeting of
minds.

What I am calling the fantasy definition of the American
Character has none of these qualities. Its own most englob-
ing quality is that it is really something that exists outside
of us but in such a way as to exert enormous pressure on
the American interior. At any rate it represents the real
wishes of nobody. It is a construct that is imposed from the
outside. Like so many other things in our civilization, it
operates as an independent mechanism or dynamism outside
of our own true characters, a mechanism with laws of its
own which, reputedly, we must respect and about which we
can do nothing. I am not going to give an important example at this stage. Let me give a simple metaphorical example. I simply imagine a cocktail party none of whose
members wishes to be there, all of whom are there to satisfy
the ghostly wishes of somebody else there who is himself not
pleased by being there. The whole process may be described
by the word *anonymity*. Nobody can come to terms or grips
with the decision because nobody has made it or wants it.
Let us imagine that everybody is putting the matter in the
mind of someone else. No one pauses to locate his own feelings, wishes or thoughts. We can call it, for that time and
for that situation, a depersonalized group. *This kind* of decision and way of action is a situation floating in the air outside of man. And as it was not in the first place produced
by the locatable thought or feeling of anyone, now, as a
separate, independent mechanism, it has the power of so
reacting back on the individual as to make even more difficult the pinpointing of his own wishes. It adds another

degree of depersonalization. These things happen to everybody. But we have to ask ourselves, what is the national
degree of occurrence? As with mental illness itself, which
differs in no way from health save in degree, the matter of
degree is critical. Especially when the situation and decision
suffering under such anonymous construction is often the
very nature of the American Character. For this question
affects not only our exterior world; it affects the deep interior of all of us. Not only does it ask the question, how
do Americans act? It also—in this order of anonymity, independent mechanism and demand—asks the question, what
should I think and feel and wish? If the boundaries of this
process of definition are growing, then we are in a bad way.
There are many people who think we are, and I am one
of them.

THE TWO CONSENSUSES

It seems very important, therefore, to realize that there
are two forms of consensus operating among us, two forms
of an accepted body of ideas about ourselves, which must be
kept separate at all costs. By consensus we mean a body of
ideas, attitudes and ways of doing things which characterize
and create a community. Where the consensus is real and
proceeds from the inside of a group whose individuals are
in touch with themselves, you not only have something that
is good but that is absolutely necessary for the existence of
a true community. No community was ever born of an absolute individualism merely promising that everybody would
leave everybody else alone.

The other kind of consensus is a meeting of minds outside of our minds. By now I have called it ghostly, anonymous, mechanical, and dominating. We must carefully dis-

tinguish these two forms of the meeting of minds or else we may get into the position of throwing out the good with the bad. For this second kind of consensus *is* frightening; its anonymity and power produces a feeling of helplessness which lays siege to the fundamental security of the human mind; it is liable at times to precipitate a blind reaction against itself that will throw out the true consensus with the false. Then our last state is worse than our first.

Let me use the metaphor of space to elaborate on the meaning of such a situation. Such a fantasy and anonymous definition of the American Character would, I repeat, involve a process of depersonalization. But let us admit that such a process has an action behind it, and we are the actors. To some degree we are throwing ourselves outside of ourselves and consenting to the process of living outside in space. Our identity is out there, nowhere, an infinite that cannot ever be quite grasped. A civilization can surely contribute as much as a parent to such a status for personality. So I do not exist in myself; I exist in space, anonymous, without identity. This is frightening. There is nothing to touch, not even oneself. This sense of touch is the center of human life on every level, in one form or other, and I suppose the biggest terror about space is that there is nothing to touch and no points of orientation. I do not know if we will ever go as far as the heroes of Kafka, but his images of this kind of sensibility are helpful to describe what we are talking about.

Now suppose that in reaction to such a destructive consensus as this we reject the whole notion of consensus. Then the problem of space and the accompanying terror is merely inverted. Let us grant, hypothetically and following some of the substantive lines of existential psychoanalysis, that we recover both our inward existence and identity. We no longer exist outside of ourselves in space. But we are now an atom surrounded by nothing but space. We are surrounded by an infinite, by an indeterminate in the Platonic sense of that word. There is no meeting of minds. The mind stands alone, in an infinite solitude. Then the process of reaction begins all over again. For this situation is an hypothesis that can only exist for a moment, and a hypothetical moment at that. The Romantic Hero alone can maintain this magnificent stance, and that only on paper. For human beings are on every level so essentially tactile that they have to reach out for the touch of something. What happens is that as you take away a real consensus or contact of minds you are forced to put some pure construct in its place. My assumption is, therefore, that to the degree you destroy a true ritual of a meeting of minds and actions you are forced to substitute for it a parody of itself, with a cheap consensus and conformity that exist nowhere but in space.

Thus all the violent efforts of the Romantic Hero, standing heroically on his own two feet but not on the earth— this is, of course, quite a trick—all these efforts will only increase the acceleration around a vicious circle. If, therefore, we have to do with a tactile animal who must be "in touch," it is necessary to be prudent as to how nationally we break this vicious circle of the growth of a fantasy consensus. Certainly it must be appraised, attacked, destroyed. But at the same time this real community must be explored, strengthened, re-created. We cannot live without it. The more we know it is there, the less we have to run around reassuring ourselves that it is there. I could too quickly raise a discussion of this proposition on the theological or ecclesiological levels, but I prefer first and once again to stick to a homely example, this time drawn from a little clinical experiment in the "tactile" nature of man.

The experiment, as I recall, was simple but thorough. It amounted to as complete an effort as possible to separate a

group of men from all sense contact with the outside world
and themselves. It eliminated all objects for the eyes, the
ears, the sense of touch; as far as possible a vacuum was produced for any tactile sense reactions. The final results over
a period of time, even for the best of those involved, were
various forms of severe disturbance and hallucination.

THE VACUUM OF HISTORY

This is the price to be paid for being alone in space, without any orientation, without something to touch. Now one
of the principal questions I wish to ask is the following. Is
it not true, and to what serious extent is it true, that there
has been a fantasy demand in the American air since the
beginning of our history—a demand that we stand on our
own in space, *without an essential sense of touch with history,* in a way and to a degree never or seldom placed so
demandingly on a culture before? That our problem is now
the very opposite, that our problem is that of a cheap conformity, is no indication of the contrary. In fact, my assumption has been and is that this ghostly consensus springs from
various denials of the real consensus, the real touching of
minds in history. If we had less sickness among us, we might
have less right to explore. Therefore I take up the right
to explore and ask the liberty, if necessary, to be wrong.

THE AMERICAN ADAM

My first document is literary. It is a fairly recent book by
R. W. B. Lewis called *The American Adam.* Mr. Lewis
sees the "American myth" emerging as a result of a dialogue
between three parties, the parties of Hope, of Memory and

of Irony. I shall stick to his analysis of the party of Hope, since the title of the book represents the fundamental meaning of this quite central fraction of our myth. The writer speaks of the image of

a radically new personality, the hero of the new adventure: an individual emancipated from history, happily bereft of ancestry, untouched and undefiled by the usual inheritances of family and race; an individual standing alone, self-reliant and self-propelling, ready to confront whatever awaited him with the aid of his own unique and inherent resources. It was not surprising, in a Bible-reading generation, that the new hero (in praise or disapproval) was most easily identified with Adam before the Fall. Adam was the first, the archetypal, man. His moral position was prior to experience, and in his very newness he was fundamentally innocent. The world and history lay all before him. And he was the type of creator, the poet par excellence, creating language itself by naming the elements of the scene about him. All this and more were contained in the image of the American as Adam.

Mr. Lewis points, but with deep sympathy, to the illusions and dangers of this ideal, this removal of a sense of being in touch with time and history. "America, since the age of Emerson, has been persistently a one-generation culture." He cites the sentence of De Tocqueville: "Among democratic nations each generation is a new people." And another simpler, firmer summary to the effect that in the United States "no one cares for what occurs before his time . . . In America, society seems to live from hand to mouth, like an army in the field."

But what interests me most about this book is one of its documented propositions that as a result of this attempt at rootlessness there is a sheer dullness of the unconscious repetition "of past intellectual movements among us." At all costs man has to move forward, but there is such a thing as an absolutely new man who ironically develops the trick of getting bogged down in the past, executing a smaller and smaller trajectory in the repetition of an old problem. In order to really move on there ought to be more historical signs in our memory which would read: Kilroy was here. These lines from the "First Anniversary" of John Donne are a perfect description of the New Adam:

> Prince, subject, father, son are things forgot
> For every man alone thinks he has got
> To be a Phoenix, and that there can be
> None of that kind, of which he is, but he.

What does it mean to be without a history except to be in a pure space, out of touch, and terrified? The problem I am especially interested in is expressed in the phrase by which Mr. Lewis sums up the more and more repetitious attempt at rebirth without history: "with ever slighter trajectories." Let us imagine the attempt at isolation becoming ever more repetitive, ever more frequent. One must depend on nothing, for the dependence is frightening. Now the new image is confirmed by thousands of images of the new, the very brand-new. The ideal could become that of the perfect obsolescence of all things, a civilization based on obsolescence. Everything which is must be new and shining and bright as the dawn. It used to be every generation not knowing the last. Now obsolescence is annual, and this is of course the death of quality and the death of style in life. (I wish I had a painting of the pair of old shoes by Gauguin to wave at this moment.) This is what is happening in the external world. But the acceleration of the idea in our internal world can become even more serious, with an even more perfect ideal of pace in space. I am thinking of the acceleration of the need of new sensation in each new moment. This is a grisly picture that is being painted, but it is only an effort to paint the final logic of a situation that can better be checked where we understand that final logic. Whatever the value of the myth of the New Adam, out of touch with the past or making a new beginning—and the values *are* great —all these things must be kept within their area of degree and must be integrated. The danger is that this particular drive has got out of hand and has become an autonomous, freewheeling mechanism under the control of nobody and rapidly accelerating its act of repetition. In order to avoid it, let us ask what the end could be.

1. The irony we return to constantly in such a situation is that this anti-historical man, out of touch with every generation but his own and ideally out of touch with every other Phoenix, is yet largely responsible for the production of a comforming habit that finally gives up the very identity it was intended to nourish. We might argue further that it is this very drive which, if it stays out of control, may push us more and more toward that very concept of a classless society which we rightly castigate when we see it, not in ourselves, but projected among our enemies. A true class is a long product of history and nature, the careful articulation of a group or an idea or a profession or a vocation. It should be an agreement based on nature, not a nature based on agreement. Our culture needs a pluralism of such groups, not simply one group to which all aspire to belong. And if asked for a simple reason for this, I think of the very simple one that the reality of man is endlessly wide. He has legs and sometimes they get him on a track team; ears for music; hands to become a surgeon or an artist or a craftsman; a mind to calculate on anything; endless forms of what Cardinal Newman would call that illative sense which is a special gift in every man. The view of history as that which is dead

is not very discerning. History is also a creative process of discovering and establishing all these realities as valid and acceptable notes for men to be and play. The more it is seen in this light, the less rigidifying will it also be seen to be. For it will also be seen as ever open to new constructs, new realities, new groups. There will then be more room than there is now for new Adams, who will take the first steps toward the formation of new groups, with the sanction of all that part of our history which is creative and acceptable to us.

2. Thus we must keep the idea of Adam versus history under perpetual surveillance, and not let the opposition between the two become a destructive catchword. For it can be destructive. Two examples come to mind:

a) The indiscriminate use of the words "melting pot" to describe the American reality versus the European past. Obviously there was an idea and a value behind it. But were the fantasy and the reality in it held under adequate examination? Why was it so completely necessary that the immigrant groups give up their past, their different cultures, their prides and self-respects? It will be a blessed day for this country when we regain a solid degree of these pluralisms. It would be wonderful to look forward to the day when people are proud of having an accent, proud of the music and images *their* history created, proud of their fathers. Is it possible that the father image is so much in the air because we have been too much asked to give it up and because we actually do not have such a real image behind our reality? Is it possible that it is precisely our abandonment of the concept of history that allows the strongest groups to keep walking into our midst with their abstract and destructive understanding of Americanism and nativism, so full of fear and hatred of every outsider? If we create a vacuum something is going to fill it.

b) "The right of everybody to go to college" is another example of the need of a criticism of terms. Our fathers did not have the right and they meant their sons to have this chance to be born anew, to move into this new class of college-goers. But what a price a large fraction of them are paying for the right to crash into a new class, to be Adam in a land of educational opportunity. The education established by the Greeks to help a man to come to self-knowledge and a knowledge of the world tends now to become a thing wherein often a man cannot find himself or his own talents, only a place where he can belong to a new class transcending all other classes. This is fine and I am not sympathetic with *all* the criticism of belonging. In fact this paper is based on the physiological as well as the theological assumption that men have to belong to something. But who anonymously sets up the terms? Who set up *these* college terms? Would it not be better to pluralize the idea with the addition of every manner of junior college, based on all the varying realities of men's talents, so that they might truly find themselves and their own creative sense? Then a man can really become a New Adam, not a hocus-pocus New Adam, yielding to somebody else's definition of the New Adam—a previously constructed definition with which our Adam has nothing to do, a somebody else on whom no one can place the finger.

MORALISM

I should like to point out another problem area that will continue to develop if we continue to abandon our dependence on, our sense of touch with, history. It is a more critical point for our mental and spiritual health than all the others. It amounts to this as a proposition: that if we go beyond reason in abandoning what history has already worked out for us, then we will come to the point of such an excess of moralism and anxious morality as will indeed endanger our most inward well-being. This, I suppose, is an unusual theological remark. But I believe it is true and I would like to explain it.

Where nothing is settled or worked out, where everything is new, then we are in the position where everything must be worked out. Let me imagine a single day in my life where everything must be questioned and worked out fresh and anew, like Pallas Athena born in full bloom without a past. I must decide how to walk, how to greet a fellow human being, what to eat, the rules of grammar, the clothes to wear, the way to deal with a child, a man, a woman. A mother bringing up a baby is no longer supported by the ways of a community but is subject every day to a thousand new situations and a thousand new pieces of advice. Are we right or wrong, is she right or wrong? There is no support. Anxiety about the last moment of action and the next moment fills the air. There is a growing feeling of apprehension and the slow extension of the question of right or wrong into huge areas where such a moral question has no relevance whatsoever. This is what we might call Puritanism at its worst, and surely it is more than a coincidence that the American Puritan historians were more strident than others in their claims that America was absolutely the New Adam without any debt to past history.[1]

So much of a rejection of history requires such a daily enormous drain on our energies that there is no energy left for creativity, for the new, for the making of history. It is too great a burden to bear for any culture or for any indi-

1. It would only confuse the issue of this chapter if it should at all be understood as depending on the historical nature of the American Puritans.

vidual. It makes any degree of healthy spontaneity impossible. It makes questioning not a gift but a disease. Once again, this is all a matter of degree. Surely we must question, and I am making a plea that we keep all our major questions under surveillance. But if all is a question, if so much is a matter of anxiety and guilt, then we will have no energy left for the real questions.

A good deal of the quality and purposes of history has nothing to do with morality, with right and wrong. It is largely a free determination of a way of life, a way of doing things, created over a sufficient period of time to allow testing and avoid compulsion. I am talking of that kind of biological consensus by which we determine the features according to which we live in relation to one another in time and space. Ideally the process is open and flexible enough to allow for change and all the possible comedy of difference within limits which can only be determined by intuition (and sometimes by the police). But my present focus is on that quality in it which keeps it removed from morality. It could have taken a thousand other forms. It is a free and not a moral choice; it is not an absolute. The important thing is not that the mother should do exactly the right thing but that, as Erik Erikson says, the baby should have the impression she knows what she is about and is not perpetually communicating anxiety. Thus she will certainly communicate anxiety if she is the totally New Eve at every moment, about to be joined at suppertime by a totally New Adam. A final caricature of the logic of this situation would of course be that it is not the same Adam who meets the same Eve of the same morning, and no doubt this would be even more confusing for the baby. So another human being goes into the world, testing everything to see if anything has been worked out, to find out if anything and everything is right or wrong.

We should not criticize the men who are trying to do without history. We should recognize that they are trying to carry too great a burden.

Therefore, we do not have a reasonable attachment to history if the trajectory of the new gets shorter and shorter. If the idea of the New Adam gets out of hand, the final consequences should be predictable: (1) a growth of anxiety as to how to deal with the most elementary facts of life; (2) a diseased extension of the moral and self-examining part of life; (3) a corresponding diminution of the areas of biological and psychological spontaneity; (4) a diseased extension of the questioning and distrust of each other—granted that we will no longer be sure of the basic and elementary reactions of all the other Adams; (5) an increase in our subjection to external forces, manipulation, and leaderships, all of the kinds that take over in the absence of a consensus slowly carved out by the internal agreement of a set of free spirits.

No matter if the answers be discouraging and a bit frightening; we should explore and fumble toward the reasons behind this growing negativity in our relationship to history. I am in no position to give a "scientific" explanation, and I wonder who is. If my thoughts do not coincide with a good number of reasonable men, so much the worse for me. If they do, they can rise to the level of the scientific. Here then are some of them as I, one man, reach for some explanations:

1. There is, as I have already tried to show, an all-or-nothing mentally among us which hungers for pure and clear ideas, untouched by complication or contrariety. Some people call it angelism. In the American context it undoubtedly has a good deal to do with puritanism. Some simple examples occur. In order that there be unity among us there cannot be difference. In order that there be free enterprise there cannot be any external influences brought to bear upon television to produce a representative fraction of quality in

its vast wasteland. That the press may be free it must be totally free in a sense that excludes the terrible burden of responsibility and reasonableness. There is an almost paranoic response to most requests for public discussions of these problems. Surely one of the marks of adulthood is to become aware that not everything is an either-or, that in fact and without compromise the most of life is a both-and rather than an either-or. I believe that the roots of a good deal of mental illness may be discovered in the unreasonable and final extension of the either-or quality of life into the areas of the both-and.

A total life of either-or is too demanding. It imposes too great a burden on people. This is notably true of history when we anonymously demand that a human being be American and a New Adam, and nothing else; that is, that he give up his history and the history of his father as though the surrender were required by the goal. To be new he is asked to be brand new. Past and future get to be an absolute either-or.

This is not just another either-or. It is central and critical, because, after all, life is full of contrariety and complications and both-ands. It takes time to work them out and into each other, so that without history the New Adams get into the position of starting all over again, tackling enormous problems as though they have never been heard of before by the human race.

What lies behind this kind of rejection of and fear of the past? Is it that we cannot think of or do not possess any form of the past that does not have impurity or corruption in it? Are we like children hungering after some Paradisical form of the pure and the clear idea? Is it that we think that the future we are about to make will never at last become such a past? But it always does, most certainly. And the danger is, as the trajectory becomes always smaller, that the discovery of reality will be accompanied by a greater wave of fantasy, a greater wave of shock, a more intense longing for a purity of situation.

2. "Is there also a fear of passivity behind the freewheeling complex which inclines to reject the past? Our history is more than something that is adulterated. It is also, like human existence itself, an achievement and a gift with which we have had nothing to do. In the face of it we are in the position of receiving, and of not taking the whole dreadful burden of action upon ourselves. Receiving is half of life, and action is only the other half. We seem to find great difficulty in receiving, equating it, no doubt, with doing nothing. But receiving, too, is one of the great acts of the human spirit. I conceive that one of the central texts of Christianity is: Let us love God who hath first loved us.

3. No doubt all history is adulterated and has involved mistakes. But the question comes to the mind, Do we incline to reject adulterated history because we cannot stand making mistakes ourselves? The inability to make and accept mistakes leads to the distortion of mistakes and the distortion of their opposites. The poles this spirituality will make us swing between are the poles of "fiasco" and "triumph." Long-term campaigns, like life itself, involve both progress and mistakes. We are therefore usually superb fighters of battles, but not good at campaigns. Our political campaigns tend more and more to become intense, strenuous battles leaving all involved exhausted. Another question is, Have we the spiritual equipment to settle down to a fifty year "campaign" of handling the modern world? Or shall we demand of every administration that it win the "battle"?

All these remarks are based on the assumption that reality, and particularly the human reality, is complicated, full of contrariety, and not pure or clear in the Cartesian sense of these words. The opposite assumption would be and is that wherever there is a situation in which we face contrariety we must choose one of the contraries involved. Such an assumption must in all logic lead to a good deal of repression or the denial of the half of the human nature. If we must choose between being dependent or independent, we are in a very bad way indeed. The clinical people are making it clearer to us that if this is the structure of our choices we are well on the way to a peptic ulcer civilization. Such is also the case for a culture too intent on a savage choice between the past and the future. The consequences of other equally savage—and equally false—choices we shall take up in the next chapter.

Finally I must yield to the temptation of making a few remarks about the present status of a few points in the Protestant-Catholic dialogue of some of these matters.

Looking back on what I have said, I notice that practically my whole argument has been based on such instinctive ruminations as a protest against the over-extension of the clear idea and the either-or or moralistic mentalities, as well as a defense of a metaphysics and theology based on the idea of the interpenetration of contraries and the complicated nature of reality. This—I have no hesitation about it—has been a normal quality of Catholic dialectic in history. On the other hand I have the impression, though it will be countered, that many traditional forms of the Protestant dialectic had moved too much toward the dialectic of the clear and unpolluted idea. The battle about the nature of the Church is a prime example. The Catholic theologian—whether in your mind he has been successful or unsuccessful at it—has always kept together the twin concepts of sin and sinlessness in his definition of the Church, and he does not let the one prevent the other. The more Protestant theologians have always been traditionally shocked by the idea that a sinful fact could also be sinless and divine. I have also in this paper suggested a number of puritan inclinations in the direction of the pure idea.

These things are not said to arouse controversy, I assure you. My purpose rather is to accentuate a certain irony that exists at the heart of some of what we may call the implications of the present moment of dialogue. It seems to me that now the implications, the impressions often created, by the two roles, Protestant and Catholic, have reversed each other. I am not necessarily talking so much about the facts as the way in which the position of each is now *understood*. The Catholic thinker is understood as defending a natural-law theory of life, and this is tasted by the Protestant as rigidly, externally and definitively conceived, as non-historical and looking to some kind of pure construct called pure reason, as having scant regard for the complications of life. Reversely, the Protestant thinker is often *understood* as protesting against such rigidity, such externalism, such purity in thinking, and is accused by some of his Catholic brethren as going too far in defending a necessary ambiguity in all things finite and human. He is often *understood* as proposing a dialectic that inhibits decision and commitment.

There is a real need of bringing these two positions into a clearer self-illumination and possibly a deeper contiguity. We must leave it to our Protestant friends in the years ahead to analyze and clarify the dialectic of ambiguity and complication. Catholic thinkers have the equal obligation of giving further clarification to their theories of the natural law, in such a way that these elements of human life we call freedom, subjectivity, historicity, complication, and contrariety are attached to it with greater clarity than at present. To some degree my own remarks in this paper on the American Character have been a slight attempt in this direction.

God knows the American character needs our common help at this moment in time. He does not have to theorize about the actuality of confusion and complication. He is in it, up to his ears. A theory or theology of pure complication will not help him. Neither will many dangerous theories of the simplistic or the many simplistic notions of Americanism. On the whole the idea of the American Adam, with his overly pure handling of our history and our pluralism, has sinned in this direction.

I have only one other thing to add here, and I mean it as a kind of summary. I have no particular love of complication and I tend to agree with those who distrust the love of it for its own sake. I have no sympathy for the literary professionals in irony who are warning us against believing that anything may mean something definite. I think that simplicity is a fine thing. And this is where history comes in. It is complication indeed, but not for its own sake. It is plain hard work toward simplicity, working at the problem of national identity, with blood and sweat and tears. The abstract intelligence can retort that history could have been otherwise and is not an absolute, but I would propose that that is to miss the point.

What strikes me as an ideal attitude toward our history is the attitude of an absolute dedication toward a history that is seen as ours but as not an absolute. Only thus will it be seen as freely chosen and only thus will we be able to respect other histories, the unity of our pluralisms in the United States, and the possibility of the extension of that idea into a unity of the free but different nations. The two ideas of history I have been trying to put together are those of the absolute and the free. And the things I have been trying to avoid are the suffering and the anxiety that characterize the moralism, the absolutism, of a non-historical civilization that like Adam is always starting anew. A non-historical culture can end up conformist, moralistic and with a style of life that can only be characterized as a lack of style. Such a fraudulent consensus feeds on any weakness in a real, historical consensus.

3

DIVIDED WE STAND

I should like to begin this chapter with a warning that has been voiced by many serious people before I ever thought to voice it. The warning would be (1) that we do indeed have a problem of divisiveness on our hands, a problem that potentially is serious, and (2) that if this critical question is not solved, and well solved, in the United States, it is not likely to be solved for our civilization in the West.

From the beginning we have in this country been a kind of testing ground for the great question whether all the bewilderingly diverse and confusing elements of modern man and modern civilization can come together into one place and together survive. The world has instinctively felt, and it is true, that we have in the providence of God and history been given a fresh start, and it has, with various degrees of preoccupation, been watching the American experiment for nearly two centuries to see what would come out of it. Now at this moment, the majority of the nations are faced with extra strains and sources of diffidence about themselves; more than ever, therefore, they are preoccupied with the condition of things in the United States; possibly it is their very anxiety about us that makes them project many of our passing affairs like the McCarthy—anti-McCarthy battle into giant, hysterical conflicts. For, despite frequent surface impressions to the contrary, I adopt the assumption here that they wish us to succeed, so central are we to the whole course and history of contemporary man.

Moreover, we have ourselves been concerned from our beginnings to strike with bold strokes at the very essence of the modern problem of unity in civilization, and have boldly announced our capacity to become a "melting pot" (I do not altogether like this phrase for the reasons given in the previous chapter). But at any rate, even beneath the superficialties of this slogan there lies the essence of a dream and ambition to bring many tongues and things together into one place and have all live lives, not of conformity, but of unity.

We have been so successful that perhaps our greatest fault in recent generations is that we have been inclined a little too much to fall back on what I would call a *magical* concept of the whole process of American unity and survival. Now the very heart of all magic is that it is a process that takes place outside of ourselves, we do not have to work at the business, carefully executed detail does not matter, we do not have to be concerned about the relation of exhausting effort, as cause, to the desired goal and effect of unity and survival. We are inclined to think of the American Republic as Catholics do of the Catholic Church: it is there and always will be; we have a kind of word of God for it. He who suggests the possibility of the opposite, of serious internal accidents, of the sort of decline that has overtaken every great civilization, is either a fool, a knave, or a traitor.

I have no intention whatsoever of voicing grave concern at our divisive predicament of this precise moment. Certainly it would be the most exaggerated and dangerous kind of rhetoric to say that our present situation has any resemblance to the difficult situation of the French Republic, where complete political divisiveness and a consequent loss of constitutional morale seem to have become national political traits. In fact it is astonishing how much our problem differs from that of the French; it is true that the quarrel between the Socialists and the Catholics on the religious level is often profound and exasperating, and is an important part of France's political divisions. But France does notoriously have a highly unified and traditional culture of the mind, complicated and sophisticated but very much all of one piece. Still this has not been enough to insure political unity and stability in recent critical moments. We, on the other hand, have never been of one cultural piece or pattern; yet this has been no obstacle to a truly amazing stability on the level of the political. Indeed, it is more than possible, as I shall later suggest, that any overly precipitate attempt to produce a common national culture on all levels of the intelligence and on all levels of the human personality may be precisely the thing to hasten the day—if ever, God forbid, it is to come—of political disunity and instability. I say so much so far only to indicate quickly that the issue of unity, and the way it is to be preserved or produced, varies incredibly from nation to nation and is not a question to be tackled by some world observer with a univocal mind.

No, we do not have an immediately grave problem on our hands. That having been said and acknowledged, there are, nevertheless, a set of emerging factors tending toward divisiveness in our day that begin to coalesce into what is, for the United States, an unusual pattern and of unusual intensity, one that should be a cause of worry for all men of good will.

I am going to suggest, as an outline of my remarks, that there are two mentalities among us that are of their very nature divisive. Before we get down to the actual business of looking at some of those concrete elements of our question in which these two mentalities are presently involved, let me make a very brief attempt at an analysis of the philosophical roots of each of them. For it is safe to say that no serious distortion in the world of action, whether in the personality of the individual or society as a whole, is without its metaphysical roots and causes.

The first divisive mentality is what I have termed the mentality of the clear idea, borrowing that term from its Cartesian and more modern context. In effect (I quote from Harmelin's *Le Système de Descartes*, Paris, 1921, p. 285), "according to the Cartesian definition of distinction and confusion (Princ. 1, art. 45, 46) an idea is confused when, instead of having precise and limited boundaries, it spreads over neighboring ideas or allows itself to be invaded by them." Thus a "clear idea" does not allow itself to be interpenetrated by any other idea; it wishes to remain decisively itself and unpolluted by anything save its own self and its own resulting clarity. In the context in which we are using the phrase, it is a generator of easy passions and partisanship, and wishes to spare itself the effort of thought that is involved in relating itself to other ideas.

In order that the meaning of this process of thinking by "clear ideas" may be unmistakable, let us begin with the highly concrete example of the issue of nationalism versus internationalism. Now there is hardly another subject that has so much occupied the popes of the twentieth century, and especially the pontificate of Pius XII. Out of that necessary preoccupation has come a long series of firm but carefully worked messages on the absolute necessity of an international order, and on all those ways in which this new venture of mankind may and must safeguard all the subsidiary relations that exist among men, ranging from individual national entities and cultures to minorities within those societies or to the rights of the individual persons within them. In its totality this papal doctrine is a careful avoidance of the two extremes of what it calls "mechanical unitarism" in a one-world culture or state and national isolationism and selfishness. Everywhere there is an insistence, though this language is not used, that neither nationalism nor internationalism may exist in the form of an absolutely clear Cartesian idea, but that the two must and can interpenetrate each other.

It is only by completely isolating one such idea from the other and allowing each to confront the other as two exaggerated straw men, as two enemies instead of two friendly ideas, that partisanship and divisiveness are built up around them. Many among us have decided that there is an eternal enmity between the two.

There is a species of nationalist and isolationist who sees the nation as a good thing (which, to put it mildly, it surely is), and lets the matter go at that. That is the end of all thinking on the subject. They thereupon proceed to assault the idea of internationalism on every front. The United Nations is not analyzed with a qualified criticism; it is simply assaulted. The idea of international organization, which has been demanded in the strongest terms by the Papacy, is condemned as one-worldism and an attack on national sovereignty. We must take a unilateral stand on everything. Use such organizations as long as they will be pliable in our hands, but God help the first day they vote against what seems to be our immediate interest. Help to other nations is a form of softheaded folly. We are so strong and so just and so right that we can afford to go it alone. This is the first straw man and the first clear idea.

On the other hand, unfortunately, there are internationalists who are completely univocal and simplistic in their thinking and plans for world unity. They are guilty of what

Pius XII, in his message to the World Federalists in 1951, called the vice of "mechanical unitarism." Under the force of their simplifying vision of this vice, all the actualities that we love, all the immediate and subsidiary realities and unities that we love—in the human person, the family, properly defined national sovereignty, native cultures—would have to be melted down into a single, world melting pot. The nation and individual cultures are an outmoded anachronism. There are also, of course, the mechanical versions of international unitarism proposed by the communists and the socialists.

My own point is that all such pairs of ideas should invade each other's boundaries, constantly, perpetually, in some way from morning to night, being mutually interpenetrating, the one nourishing the other, each as it were creating the other. And my further point is that this fusion requires constant thought of the most difficult kind, constant effort, constant discipline, if they are to be kept together and in the right balance.

Now, contrarily, look what happens if this synthesis is broken down and we become enamoured of either member of this pair to the exclusion of the other. The human being is easily fascinated by the power and clarity of the clear idea. Instead of disciplined thought and effort, it involves a letting oneself go, a freewheeling emotionalism. In addition to having a passionate cause as object of all your energies, say freedom or authority (it is always an either/or), you also have the incredible advantage of an object for your hatreds. Two things that should support each other have become enemies. Slowly the process of polarization intensifies itself. The nationalism versus internationalism debate is only one such issue. Pairs like freedom and authority, freedom and security, tradition and progress, positive and defensive anti-Communism, even the relationship between the thinkers and the people that we may call the relation between the Body and the Mind of society—all these interpenetrating pairs begin to break down and to fall apart, each member of each pair, into an isolated existence. Each element goes off to its extreme corner or pole, and insists that its brother idea be isolated at another extreme pole where it can be viewed with hostility and fear. The extremists have gone to work. The traditionalists will have nothing to do with change, and defend the status quo with passion; the man of change will have nothing to do with tradition. Many of those who are properly concerned with investigating Communism will stubbornly and stupidly suspect positive anti-Communism of being communistic.

Through this separation each distorts an idea into an unhappy and easily attackable form. And both attack the men of the center, demanding that they speak out and join one extreme or other. You begin to be offered all kinds of rigid dichotomies. Even a stalwart figure like Whittaker Chambers, admirable in so many ways, seemed to offer us nothing but the choice between a fight for God and a fight for man; though the Catholic instinct is never to separate these two great fields of combat, but rather to unite them inseparably in the one act. All these dichotomies represent some elements of the classical division between the Right and the Left.

As another example, take the matter of the conflict between the partisans of freedom and the partisans of security in the nation a few years back. It was of course only the latest version, albeit intensely passionate and emotional, of the age-old problem of the relation between freedom and authority, the person and society. It is simple enough to become a partisan of one or the other, and thus seek safety in the numbers and approval of your party. You decide that the relationship is a dichotomy, one of separation and hostility.

A further example would be the tendency of the most of

us in varying degrees to burrow within one's own group, to become lost in a single category of society, and, over against the common good, to seek only the interest of this separated and clear idea: whether it be the idea of big labor or big business or big agriculture or that of the white-collar middle class. Over against this tendency we must be perpetually reminding ourselves that there is a Christian and magnificent conception of politics, founded on our unity as human persons seeking the organic common good, and a degenerative form of politics which, after the fashion of a private lobby with one clear idea, seeks only the interest of the group or category to which one belongs on the more superficial levels of the human person. This is beginning to be that kind of political period; we all begin to belong to categories, to burrow in our foxholes and shoot at people in other categories.

We can afford to spend a little more time in the analysis of a fourth example of the divisiveness produced by the philosophy of the clear idea, because it is probably far more fundamental than the others and perhaps lies at the root of many of them. I am thinking of the existence of the two widely separated cultures among us, the intellectual and the popular culture, and of the now long standing abyss that exists between society and those we might call the intellectuals.[1]

As a matter of fact there *is* such a division of culture today. We are faced, and have for most of this century been faced, with the existence of two cultures in this land, the one diametrically opposed to the other and the two facing each other with something that resembles hostility—certainly, to put it very mildly, with a complete failure of contact. The one, the culture of the few, is something that tends to an isolated, attenuated and overly sophisticated form, to a poetry

1. This division is considered from another perspective in Chapter Five, "Culture and Belief."

and an art that smacks of a secret cabalistic quality of self-expression. The other, the culture of the masses, the culture of Hollywood, the crooner and all the cheaper forms of mysticism for the people, is largely an artificial concoction that has, by a new business of art, been thrust down the throats of otherwise good people. Never, at any rate, has there been such an abysmal gap between the many and those who by vocation should be its creative and imaginative leaders. The two groups, like two armed factions, look upon each other with great mutual distrust.

Then there is the chasm that grew up in the twenties of this century between society itself and the intellectuals. The astonishing rush and development of the country's industrial power after the First World War began to be accompanied by a mass attack of the creative writers, bitter and unqualified, on the cultural pattern they conceived to belong to that development. There are the names of Theodore Dreiser, Sinclair Lewis, Scott Fitzgerald, Ring Lardner, Thomas Wolfe, James T. Farrell, John Dos Passos, Erskine Caldwell, William Faulkner, John Marquand, and many others. There are the provocative themes used by such names: the themes of cynicism and disillusionment, the attack on the business man and on the ordinary man, the bourgeois; the criticism of selfish power and exploitation, of cheapness, vulgarity and mediocrity; the blasts against the injustices of our economy. It was all summed up in three lines by Archibald MacLeish in his dramatic poem "Panic":

> Blight—not on the grain
> Drought—not in the spring
> Rot—not from the rain

And it has all come, of course, to be summed up by the well-worn word "alienation," a word coined to describe the abyss between the intellectual and society and the fact that they do not belong the one to the other. I take the summarizing sentence from Henry Steele Commager's *The American Mind* (pp. 248–249): "Never before in American literature and rarely in the literature of any country had the major writers been so sharply estranged from the society which sustained them. . . ."

There are many senses in which that difficult period is over and done with in American life. Great victories were won in the name of social justice. American capitalism is no longer the thing it was, and no longer the thing that ignorance and distance still allow a large segment of the European continent to think it is. In many ways it has come to maturity, and the growth of our money system away from the ideas of selfishness and exploitation toward ideals of generosity and public service, though far from perfect, has been truly astonishing in this short time. And if we are to place stock in the mid-century symposium conducted by the *Partisan Review* among the writers, there is much more sympathy with the ordinary citizen and with the homely realities of American life.

Nevertheless this history of revolt and alienation has left its scars and still has its aftermath. There is now a tradition of alienation, of criticism and non-conformity, among the writers and intellectuals. And while that is all right, while there will always be a necessity for protest and criticism and courage against mob views, there is some danger that this spirit of freedom from society and non-conformism will become the *central* tradition of many of our thinkers, writers and university people. I say *danger* because the central tradition of the intelligence in human society should be that of a kind of natural priesthood of light, communicating light and guidance to the people, leading the people and not itself to the heights of freedom and truth. We may well raise the question today whether the actual ideal that is sometimes raised for the American university man and thinker and writer is not that of the isolated romantic hero who thinks that his own salvation, his own freedom, his own sincerity, are the only things that matter, and the devil take the people. Once again let us acknowledge that intellectual and academic freedom are terribly important matters, and let us be honest enough to say that the people have themselves not been guiltless of the charge of anti-intellectualism. That having been said quite clearly, then let us say again, and firmly, that we are faced with the possible development of a permanent and dangerous intellectual tradition in America, one which would transfer a purely peripheral question of the right of protest and rebellion to a place of complete centrality in the vocation of the thinker and onetime guide of civilization. I say this as one who is intensely convinced that the people need the intellectuals.

The form of divisiveness that would result from all this could not be more serious. For it would mean nothing less than a division between the body and mind of our society.

No one man can presume to know what advice God would at this moment give to these two factions, and only God can speak perfectly, with a clear mind that would be without prejudice to either camp. Nevertheless, we who have dark and finite minds must occasionally make the attempt at judgment and the giving of advice. Thus we might formulate the following pieces of counsel for the few and for the many.

For the few: in this state of tension and distrust and mutual incomprehension, you must remember that you are especially blessed with light and should be with strength. You must therefore be the first to yield to the necessity the others, the many, have for sympathy and understanding. We are not asking you to give up your right to courage and criticism and free speech (God help the society that is without these virtues); but you must remember that culturally and spiritually the people are in a tragic situation that cannot be resolved without your help. You are too fastidious about cheapness and vulgarity, and easily forget that no human soul asks for these vices but has them foisted upon him. You are always talking about your alienation from society and your sensitive abandonment, but you must also remember that it is often you who have abandoned the people and left them to their own resources. At the first sign of a rebuff you fled from them, like sensitive children. You always have the air of speaking from the outside, as though you did not belong to the people, as though you were yourselves without guilt. A generation ago, when the problem of the nation was social injustice and the mood was social progress, you found yourselves allied with a vast bulk of the Christian and religious forces of the country and were emboldened by your mutual success. Today the problem and the agony faced by the people are intensely greater than the social question; the problem is one of survival and existence itself, and the anxieties that come from facing the very deepest planes of existence. The liberal intelligence has been accused very often of being without those inward resources of the mind and the spirit that would enable it to handle the true tragic question, the question of death and human finitude with which we are now confronted. You have concentrated on the question of life and progress, and the question of freedom *on these levels,* and have achieved extraordinary successes there, and a temporary unity with the Christian conscience. Since the end of the seventeenth century, when you began to overthrow the classical order of the static and the status quo, all your victories—and I do not underestimate the importance of many of them— have been on the level of the political and the social and the temporal. Now you are not being asked to give up any of these desires, but you *are* being asked to go deeper and higher as well, where you may again in unity meet the conscience and needs of a people who are stricken as they have never been stricken before. Thus, where you stood on common ground with many of the people a generation ago, you do not today possess with them a common language. And thus, in this context where you continue to rely on solving the tragic question on a predominantly political level, even your most legitimate concerns about political freedom and social progress run the risk of being misunderstood. Courage is a magnificent virtue, and you must always follow your conscience, but do not insist too much on putting all your eggs, so to speak, in the same basket, the basket of courage and attacks upon the people. There is also the need of humility, a desire to analyse the people from within and not upbraid from without, and a new willingness to contact the true desires and fears of the people in a day such as ours, when reality and being in all its amplitude must become the true subject for debate. Until you consent to do this, there will always be a vacuum of leadership among the many, into which will always rush leaders whom you do not like. The result will perpetually be that the divisiveness we have been talking about will be exacerbated because you will then yield to the temptation of devoting all your energies to fighting these leaders instead of tackling from the inside the true and profoundly intellectual problems of the people. But it is you who, from your vantage point, on the outside, of personal salvation and strength, will have helped to create the vacuum. Then the divisiveness will go from worse to worse, and it is this form of it that, I suspect, will always lie at the heart of the more superficial forms of divisiveness which we have mentioned before.

As for the many: in what we have been saying of the few, we do not intend to exonerate the many or to excuse them from their responsibilities in any crisis of division. The very essence of a democracy, it seems to me, is that within it responsibility is distributed on as broad and complete a base as possible. Democracy is marked by a spirituality that will not tolerate the ordinary citizen's identification of himself with a mass or a mass-culture and an avoidance of responsibility for what he has become or for what the nation has become. It is, according to the Christmas message of Pius XII in 1944, precisely the kind of policy that, as an organic order of interiorly responsible and self-actuating individuals, is most opposed to the machine concept of the *mass* or collectivity which allows itself to be blown in every direction and manipulated from the outside; by self-interested leaders, by propaganda, by cultural fads, by giant waves of unpredictable emotions, by passion, by sex, by glib columnists, by everything save themselves and their own judgments—which should be self-originating, though illuminated by facts and real understanding. The people have no right to band together in a formless mass, as a kind of self-protection for all and a common, consoling defense, against the light of the intelligence and a true culture, branding all who would criticize them, or help them, as eggheads and do-gooders and bleeding hearts. They have no right, before God or man, to become anti-intellectual. For they have the native light of natural instincts and intelligence which have always in times past been able to produce healthy popular cultures, based on native customs, family life, good music, healthy if unsophisticated manners, religious symbols, and, finally, all the natural community ties that come from being bound together on the profoundest planes of life and death. Because they distrust, and rightly so, some among those we have been calling the few, this does not mean they have the right to call the many magically right, and thus dispense with all self-criticism, picking only those leaders who will flatter them and those elements of culture which will appeal to the least thoughtful parts of the human personality.

Now I am not at all sure that precisely this version of
division and hostility which exist between the few and the
many is necessarily the basic and the most important version
of our American problem of divisiveness. It may very well
be that it is, but debate on that subject will get nowhere. I
wish rather to take it as an example of a general principle that
I am driving at in this discussion. We must not be pushed,
through our criticism of any one group in society, into complete and unalloyed and absolute sympathy and devotion to
another. Nor because of the criticism of any one absolute
ideal must we allow ourselves to be driven into exclusive
devotion to its opposite. This is not at all to take a compromising and middle-of-the-road position; it does not at all
mean that we refuse our dedication to a clear-cut stand or to
any absolute principle. It does mean that we recognize that
unity is a terribly difficult thing, always a matter of putting
contraries together, never a univocal matter of taking an
overly simple and partisan solution such as inevitably leads
to class warfare. He who exclusively adopts either party and
its present state of being has either given up thinking or
desires popularity. He is certainly being led by the easy
enthusiasm generated by the clear idea.

In sum, then, there is a desperate need that the Mind and
the Body of society, the intellectuals and the people, not
permit their suspicions of each other to grow. The thinkers
must live within the people, not in such a way that they
accept all their ideals, manners and morals but in such a
way, after Christ himself, that they become concerned and
illuminating forces from within. And here we must insert
a warning.

There is a group of intellectuals in this country, though
perhaps not usually denominated such, who are indeed concerned about the people and most interested in them. They
are trying to influence the people, down to the least thought

and the least stirring of the human heart. Thus they are not spiritually alienated and non-conformists as these others are. But despite this zealous concern they indeed live, in a very important sense, on the outside of the people, and, if anything, they will constitute a greater spiritual problem to society than these others, because they tend to be accepted completely by the people.

I am thinking of the social and the psychological and the cultural and the educational engineers in our midst, men with a simple pattern of life for all of us on their brain. They are the artificial concocters of that kind of automaton and robot civilization which affects the imagination, the eyes, the ears, the walk, the speech, the habits of all of us in a constant and insidious way all the day long. I am thinking of the planners, manipulators, engineers of our popular mores and culture, the entertainment industry, the columnists many of them, the advertisers many of them, who are teaching us how to react to every situation in life. I am thinking of the problem of the modern job that does not allow for the creative spirit of the human person. And there is the growth of the modern business corporation which, though it has come to such generous maturity, now inclines with an overly generous paternalism to adopt the human person into itself as into the real and ultimate family of our modern city, claiming the loyalty and devotion to its pattern of an ever-increasing area of the human personality. There are the teachers colleges, many of them, teaching the whole man in us how to fit into a completely secular pattern of democratic living.

All these forces are forces manipulating and engineering us from the outside with stimuli, as though we were machines, reducing the responsible self-actuating, self-judging Christian soul to standardization. A true teacher, on the other hand, is a creative person who makes us think and will of ourselves from the inside; he makes us think and he makes us interiorly free.

Thus we have been very much concerned, some of us, about the non-conformist thinker and writer and the divisiveness between him and society. May I suggest we be a little more concerned to have a proper divisiveness between Christian society and this other kind of thinker whom I call the engineer and manipulator. The final struggle of Christianity will not, in this great country, be with the first, the non-conformists, but with the second, the standardizers and the non-Communist collectivizers of the human soul.

There are, therefore, different ways, some acceptable, others not so, in which the contraries, the clear ideas, can relate themselves to each other. The mind of our society can relate itself to the people in such a way that it merely manipulates from the outside. It can also act from the inside, so that intelligence interpenetrates the people in a real way, making them conscious and responsible.

There are different forms of unity, some acceptable and others not so. The Catholic Church stands passionately for American unity, but it will stand as passionately against a unity which means a standardization of the human soul and its mechanization. Against this latter kind of unity it will always finally have to be non-conformist.

But even here, even in this opposition, it will refuse to operate as an alien body from the outside. It is easy to run away from the problem of American industrial civilization and to try to resort to what the French would call the solution of integralism, to keep ourselves unspotted from this world, rather than moving into the very heart of factories and television and the theatre and the business office; perhaps we must live in the minds of the mechanizers themselves, engaging in an interior debate with them; for they too are human and who are we to adopt a new contemptuous attitude of alienation?

At the end of this all too simple discussion of the mentality of the clear idea which does not choose, or does not know how, to put opposites together, let us add one final remark. We do not mean to say that there are not contradictories in this world that will never fit together in this world or the next. There is good and evil and they will never, like the lion and the lamb, lie down together, and we must always choose partisanly between them. Communism can never be reconciled with any of the ideals of our civilization. That having been said, we can then say what every schoolboy in philosophy knows, that there is a difference between contradictories and contraries, and the latter can and must fit together, like different colors far removed from each other, into an organic spectrum, if we are to have a truly organic unity.

The second principal source of divisiveness among us, I suggest, is the presence of what we may again call the univocal mind in our American civilization.

Now, if you will remember, a universal idea is one that finds and summarizes the common elements in many things belonging to a group or class. It is a unifying idea, and unifies by concentrating on what is the same among many and neglecting or putting aside the individual difference.

Paradoxically, it is the exclusive passion for just such unifying ideas that creates divisiveness among us. It decides that there is a least common denominator of sameness among us, and this least common denominator, this *minimum man,* is the American ideal to which all other men and things and ideas must be reduced in the name of unity. You will notice immediately how the ordinary human way of working out the problem of unity has been reversed by this univocal process. I would say that the ordinary human way is to seek the highest values and try to unify a nation around them. But with *this* univocal mentality, quite the opposite happens. A least common denominator of unity becomes the blazing ideal on every level of life, and if there is something better in the order of values and truths outside of it, so much the worse for it. It is presently not a unifying factor. Therefore out with it. You can see what would happen to religion and the things of God about which we disagree, if this mentality is pushed to its ultimate logic.

Why is this unifying mentality actually divisive? Because anything that lies outside the minimum man, outside the least common denominator, must in all logic be viewed as divisive, as alien, as an invader, literally as an enemy. If you are not completely reduced, on all the levels of the human personality, to this unifying concept, you are not an American, you are not a native, you do not belong. I believe that, in his criticism of the Catholic Church, this is the logic of Paul Blanshard who speaks, mind you, as a worried American. Reductively what I believe he is saying, whether he knows it or not, is this: there is such a thing as Americanism, not only a unity of political structure but a unity also of morals, mores, and culture. We will not tolerate any international criticism of this precise historical reality. A certain school of thought on birth control is not American; neither is the contemplative life. And the reason is that neither agrees with contemporary American mores and ways of doing things. I wonder, then, if it is not clear to you that what Mr. Blanshard is after is an incredible union of Church and State, a nationalized Catholicism—or Protestantism for that matter—which would always place its complete sanction on the Americanism of the present moment. According to this inner logic, God would have successively to be a good American in America, a good

Swiss in Switzerland, and so forth. You see how many persons there would be need for in this Trinity.

Let me pause here to make a plea for a distinction between religion as divisive and religion as analyzer and critic of American civilization. And here is a point where Catholicism and Protestantism can afford to agree and not march too hastily into unthoughtful opposition and hostility. Even more decisively than many of the intellectuals, the Catholic Church, at least on the level of American moral and spiritual life, will always, to the degree that is necessary, be non-conformist and independent. But unlike some of these, it will be non-conformist from within the people, with the withinness of a kind but intransigent father who is concerned for a family. Both its intransigence and its sympathetic withinness will be taken from the ways of Christ.

And might we not make this further plea to the different groups in this country: to the intellectuals, to our Protestant brethren, to our Jewish brethren? A plea that, where they are critics of Catholicism, they remain separately faithful to their separate identities and principles of criticism: a plea that they should not be unitedly trapped into a common criticism of the Church that would take the form of a least common denominator defense of secularism and the minimal man over against a non-conformist Church. Let them beware of *such* a common league against Catholicism, for it would mean ironically that they had accepted the principle that the intelligence and religion are essentially divisive and must never emerge as independent critics of American politics and morals and society. One more specific plea would be that they should not stand united behind the present drive of some groups in this country for an absolute and exclusive public school system that would seek to unify the country through a least common denominator education and that would call private schools, with their separate cultural and spiritual convictions, un-American, and divisive.

It is important to realize that there is all the difference in the world between the univocal mind, with its tendency to reduce everything to a minimum common culture and its demand that all differences accommodate themselves to whatever the Americanism of the moment is—between this and the mind that plunges below the surface to find what the root core of human personality is in any civilization and to build our agreements in the political order on that solid rock, the solid rock of natural law, the human person and human justice which lies below all our differences. We must remember that this kind of penetrating and not superficial act of the mind has been the basis of our political unity from the beginning, and that we have always decisively rejected as our center of unity all the more superficial categories and unities into which some other nations have fallen. Above all we have never demanded that our unity take the form of an ethnic or a racial unity, or a cultural unity.

This is so important that I repeat it. Our principle of unity is not ethnic or cultural, but wishes to penetrate below all such categories to the human person in his bedrock nature. This is why the American experiment is so vital to human history at this point, because we are a smaller experiment in what must now be achieved on the international level, a unity of disparate races, cultures, and states who must learn how to live together on a rock-bottom level of human rights if they are to survive.

There have, of course, been eruptions in our history against this fundamental American idea, but they have always finally been rejected. There was the long series of American Nativist movements, and you will recall that the Ursuline sisters had the honor of having their convent burned at such hands in Charlestown, Mass., in 1834. By 1835 the Nativist idea had

110,000 members in Massachusetts and Pennsylvania and had elected eight members of Congress on a native-American ticket. Then, to mention a few specific groups, there was the order of United Americans; in 1850 we had the emergence of the group called startlingly the Order of the Star Spangled Banner. By 1866 we had the Ku Klux Klan among us and by 1887 the famous American Protective Association (the APA). All of these groups were characterized by a narrow Americanism which they wished to define on ethnic and cultural levels for themselves and from which they would exclude all others as outsiders and aliens. Today, while we may note with joy that the vulgarities and the violence of such forms of nativism and exclusion are a thing of the past, what we have to attend to is the development of the more sophisticated forms of Americanism we have been talking about.

The two things that flash into the mind when it tries to summarize the spirituality of the univocal man take the form of two images: the first is the image of the comedian, the comic figure; the second is the potentially ruthless character, the classic character of the revolutionary. The comic character first, because the whole drive of such a figure is to proceed under the full steam of one passion or one idea and to be smashed by all the diverse realities—including stone walls, the law of gravity and other people—which simply refuse to accommodate themselves to his single-tracked mania. The comedy comes from ignoring reality. Secondly, the ruthless character: for the univocal mind is often potentially the man, like Kirilov in *The Possessed* of Dostoevski, who has such a passion for his single idea in society that he will war on all differences and pluralisms and is willing to knock off many heads to reduce society to the shape of his plan.

He has no use for difference and calls it divisive; he is a perfect logician, is intolerant, humorless, and sometimes a little mad. He is the kind of pure intellectual that true intellectualism, the student and organizer of the real, must perpetually fight against in our day.

Surely the American Catholic should himself be most careful not to be tainted with this kind of spirituality that is most opposite to his own inherited spirit. He will always, if he is truly Catholic, have a great respect for human persons and human difference. He will be, or should be, pre-eminently a man of reason, interested in fact and in truth, dominated by these and not seeking to dominate them in terms of any purely ideological decision he will have made in advance. Even if he is asked whether he is for or against the man of free enterprise, for or against the one-worlder, for or against Goldwater or Rockefeller, he will perhaps answer this in his own way: "These are not good questions; they are univocal questions, questions of personal names and narrow emotions. What is the particular case and what the particular facts in each case (only with God Himself can we identify a Name and a perfect crusade): I demand that each such question be broken down into all the separate questions each really contains, and I ask for the facts. Given the latter, I reply, with personal decision and after personal thought; I am for him on this, this, and this; against him on this, this, and this (factually, decisively, fearlessly). Which effectively means, of course, that my Catholic conscience is really never for persons but for God's truth and God's facts. Surely such a spirituality of political decision will never divide any nation; the univocal mind always will.

Let me finally add four closing principles as a kind of last word to the univocal mind:

1. There is an unbreakable relation and difference between the temporal order and the spiritual order. It is only in totalitarian countries that the spiritual order of religion is not permitted to enter, indirectly, through the consciences of men, into the city of man to analyze, criticize or guide

their actions on the temporal plane. Not only Catholics, but Jews and Protestants, must remain unitedly faithful to the proposition that to call this action of religion divisive is a totalitarian principle, even if it be enunciated within a democracy.

2. Again, there is a decisive difference between the temporal and the spiritual orders. The plane of the temporal is the area of government in this country, and it limits itself decisively to the political area. It is the area of citizenship, and of practical and complete co-operation for the temporal common good among Catholics, Protestants, Jews and non-believers. On this plane all must be one and united.

3. Within the temporal order there is and always will be room for considerable flexibility and variation of judgment as to what concrete steps are best for the attainment of the temporal common good. Once again it is precisely the kind of mind that will insist on absolute rigidity here and will not have any patience with such flexibility and variation that will produce divisiveness among us. To condemn such flexibility in religious terms will also produce the same effect. Catholics especially, therefore, with their extra clarity of principles, will hesitate more than any other group to ask for an undeviating and rigid party line in the political order. We may here remember the words of St. Paul that we were not baptized into Paul or Apollo but into Christ, and for the names Paul and Apollo and any other name of that period we might easily but reverently substitute the names of major members of the two political parties. Let the Catholic beware who will equate the Church with any politician. We cannot so wound the unity of the Body of Christ.

4. Contrarily, the American people, concerned as they rightly are for unity in the temporal order, must never artificially and irreverently demand a corresponding unity in the spiritual order. The order of the temporal common good

is one where Catholics, Protestants, Jews and non-believers must zealously unite in a human and flexible way. But the best way to avoid real divisiveness over the order of the spirit and God is to recognize, openly and honestly, that this is an area of truth and debate, where conviction alone matters. Any other attitude would be an offense to God and man and the martyrs.

4

The Problem of Freedom

One of the greatest and most enduring debates between the Christian and the non-Christian mind in our civilization revolves around the question of freedom. Now when we say that freedom (and the whole question of what creates the free soul or the free society) is an enormous matter, we mean more than that it is a point of large discussion. The truth is, rather, that modern man talks about it so much because for him it means everything. Whether or not this feeling of his is distorted is something else again, but at any rate, he does feel that freedom is the be-all and end-all of life, and he is inclined to select the Catholic as one of the imaginary foes of this powerful instinct in him.

On the other hand, the Caltholic, when he is thus so powerfully confronted with such criticism, hesitates to take up one of his own most venerable and eternal positions; namely, that freedom can indeed be greeted as *the* end of all personal and social life—that he *can* agree with his critics on this principle, and go on from there with the whole debate. Instead, he sometimes allows himself to be maneuvered into a position of suspicion and distrust, into a spirit in which he keeps reiterating and warning that liberty is only one among many values, that it is *a* facet of life—which must be watched and carefully contained. Thus he is unnecessarily trapped into an apparent hostility toward freedom and into the use of antilibertarian phrases. The net results are frequently the following: First of all, the whole controversy takes on the form of hostility versus hostility. Secondly, the secular, or at any rate the anti-Christian, position, though it regularly terminates in an incredible number of forms of slavery, is often allowed to use all the vocabulary of liberty, while the Christian, and especially the Catholic, whose whole theology is nothing but a passion for complete and endless freedom, often finds himself using a vocabulary which does not do justice to this supreme instinct of his. But thirdly and most importantly, the upshot of the whole situation is that the discussion between the two opposing groups on the role of freedom is developing on the wrong level. Such a statement leads, of course, to the simple question, What, then, is the correct level of debate? Let me suggest the answer to this question as I see it.

The answer, in terms of an initial simplicity, would amount to this: Let both parties begin by agreeing to the pre-eminence, the character as final human goal, of the idea of freedom, for this is not the critical issue between them at all. The modern man of the West is dedicated as never before, at least professedly, to the creation of all that is free, democratic, unbound. Indeed, we can and should go further by recognizing that his many professions about these things, his many social and political constructs, represent an insight and an historical development which are profoundly genuine and in many ways profoundly religious. At any rate, he unhesitatingly gives this insight and this development first place in the order of his goals.

Let the Catholic respond by accepting the same premise,

the same preoccupation, the same pre-eminent goal, for human life. Indeed, let him even surpass the secular position, as well he might, in fervor and passion—a fervor and passion which will for him be founded on the most solid kind of theological self-understanding. Let us here think of St. Paul, whose mind was surely preoccupied with the new fact of the Christian conquest of every form of slavery, and who did not hesitate to fling it forth, as a challenge of love and not of hostility, into the face of the world, into the face even of those intellectuals of Athens who thought they had a higher freedom to give than he. How simply he describes his own soul when he says: "Am I not free? Am I not an apostle?" (1 Cor. 9:1) He turns to his fellow Christians, and sums everything up with equal simplicity: "You have been called to liberty, brethren." (Gal. 5: 13) (Certainly he adds: "Only do not use liberty as an occasion for sensuality," and this must be looked into to see the full Christian picture.) Finally Paul knows, as every Christian should know, that which he aims at is a perfect, a complete, accomplishment of all things, of all his desires. He is aiming at a heavenly city. But how does he describe it? He declares that "that Jerusalem which is above, is free." (Gal. 4: 26)

Thus we have begun with a first point. So far as pure feeling is concerned, there is no basic difference in human goals between the Christian and the secular view. With all its heart *every* human heart wishes to be free, without let or hindrance of any kind, without obstacle, without limit, with fullness, abundance, and a total passion which it hopes will, in its achieving, be identical with tranquillity. Why should we in the least question this feeling? The first step we should take in solving any doubts about this secular view, be it repeated, is to go far beyond it in intensity of claim and acceptance. And let this intensity exist on every level, human as well as divine, so that we can share, and more than share, in every human and secular operation in the modern world which moves toward individual, social, cultural or political freedom. Only then, only after having examined our conscience and our heritage to see that there is no need for qualm or inhibition about freedom, need we go on to the second level of discussion on this whole burning question, for despite everything said up to this moment, we *do* feel that we have a quarrel with much of the world and its freedoms. We do know that somewhere there is a chasm of real difference, and ground for a real, at times a violent debate. The whole question is, where shall we locate the *true* controversy—locate it on such a level and in such a way that we will not run the risk of causing Christ and Christianity to be misunderstood or condemned by the world as antilibertarian—or even as antireligious! For religion, if it is anything, is the communication of freedom.

I

The real issue, the accurate level of debate, is: How shall that liberty on which we are now all agreed be achieved? And I do not think it unfair to say that (according to the Christian intelligence) as neither beauty, nor peace, nor God can be achieved save by a march through the concrete and the limited, the same thing is true of the Christian march to freedom. It is to be reached only through the finite, through facts, through limited facts, through the limits of moment after moment of time, often through the ugly, and finally through death. Nor do I mean, in saying this, that it is achieved only at the end of this path, as though freedom were a reward for having obediently submitted to remaining unfree until death. For this would certainly be not only a superficial but even a fatal view of Christian liberty. It would be equivalent to saying that that freedom which exists in the heavenly Jerusalem (which is the free city par excellence) will be given to slaves, and must therefore be looked upon as something to be leaped to from slavery. So that once more we would be in a theological world where we are always using the language of leaping, where neither heaven nor total freedom would have any roots in the earth or in the forms of earthly freedom. And we would be in the position of thinking that the liberty of Jerusalem, which, if anything is, is an interior condition, can be given to those who have not freely moved toward it, asked for it, accepted it. No, then; it may be true that freedom is a reward, but it is a reward for those who have remained free. Therefore, let us restate the Christian path to freedom. If the latter is achieved through the finite, through the homely concrete fact, then it is achieved, or achievable, in and within every such finite and every such moment. Thus the Christian is really standing by a kind of mystery in this debate; he is insisting that freedom, which is always a kind of unbounded infinite and always involves a feeling of non-limitation, is reached in the very innards of the finite and the limited. We can call this a natural mystery, for so in a sense it is. But at least it is a mystery which is ruggedly realistic; realistic because it is not so naive as to think that, when we who are small and concrete are free, this freedom, which truly gives us the sensed victory of living without bonds and without necessity, exists in some artificial way *outside of us*. The very opposite is true. The fact of being bounded and the victory of being unbound are, in man, one and the same fact, one and the same act, undifferentiated, undivided, identified. And I have called this a natural mystery, which indeed it is, because this extraordinary phenomenon has its Christian counterpart on the plane of supernatural mystery, within the reality of which the creature, the made and small one, the

baby under the stars, achieves a most complete and final freedom by an identification with the unbounded and infinite
God.

It is unnecessary to spend more than a short space on a
preliminary description of the character of the opposition to
this Christian idea of the path to liberty. As this opposition
thinks in so many other matters, so it thinks in the matter
of freedom. It cannot conceive that the contemptible concrete can be a path to so glorious a thing, or actually contain it within itself. It cannot conceive that anything but
infinite acts can in all sense lead to the unlimited achievement which it feels freedom to be. According to its religious
pattern of thinking, it not only looks toward the limited
thing as small, but also as mean, and therefore to be escaped
from. In its more purely human forms of thought, it regards
the human self in the same way, and thus, in its passion to
be free, it wishes to be free *out of this self*. For it, therefore,
liberty is really an escape, and for that reason can never be
anchored in the self, much less be identical with it.

The reader may say at this juncture: but all this is abstract
speculation and not itself very meaningful in terms of reality,
for how can a man leap out of himself and really live in a
freedom which has no roots in himself? What then is all
this talk about the other half of the world deciding to live
in an infinite outside of itself, and to proceed to freedom
through such an impossible path? Two things can be said of
such a reaction. First of all, it is, without knowing it, an
indirect confirmation of all that the Christian conscience
holds, namely, that such a process is really impossible. Secondly, the protest has some justice behind it, because thus
far we have had to be vague and abstract in our first summary of this second freedom "camp." But let us at this stage
give one example of the actual way in which this "impossible
path" is really being ventured upon. There are an endless

number of modes in which men *are* living outside of themselves in a specious attempt at freedom. They do it, they do this leaping, by moving out of the center of themselves, out of their real selves, toward the creation of specious selves which are not themselves at all. They live in the minds of others, let us say for glory's sake. And these other minds are a quasi infinite into which men enter and enter and enter with thirst and without end. They abandon the search into the true and single self which is apparently so narrow a thing, so finite, and have decided that freedom, which is always a kind of infinite, must always be found elsewhere.

There, then, stands the suggested opposition, the true opposition, the reason for a true *debate,* a violent one if necessary, and not for mere hostile *misunderstandings* as to who is or is not fighting for that pristine thing called freedom—a thing which in the minds of all of us is without price and beyond question. As the Christian need not hesitate about his first premise, neither need he about this second. For he knows that, as God himself must be found, not immediately in his immediate self, but in and through the narrow Christ, so freedom too, which gives that sense of divine universality the soul groans for, is not to be found in an overly immediate search for that fullness, but through and in a narrower way.

Thus, if in the case of our first premise we have once recurred to a Paul who has refused to modify by one inch the legitimacy of this thirst of the soul, let us recur to him again for some brief theological descriptions of this narrow way. So far we have not heard him talk about any specificities in freedom. All that we have said up to the moment is that wherever the latter truly exists he is completely for it. Therefore, I do not believe we would do justice to the Christian and Pauline position if we should conceive of him speaking or thinking in the following fashion: If a non-Christian is totally free and if a Christian is totally free, I, nevertheless, and simply because of my devotion to Christ, make choice of *Christian* liberty. This is undoubtedly the way in which most people regard the Catholic intelligence as operating, and they therefore regard it as making purely partisan choices. They think of it as saying: there is an effective secular way of being free—and, for that matter, of being or doing anything—and there is an effective Catholic way, but Catholicism simply makes an arbitrary choice of fidelity—fidelity to our own narrow community and our own narrow religious tradition. They instinctly regard us as a *camp*.

But St. Paul does not think in terms of way against way to a perfect thing, to liberty, nor does he think there are an infinite number of passages to this one, same thing. Just as we have seen on a lower level of application that for each man there is only one way to unboundedness, and that that way lies through his own concrete center, not by an *escape* into an infinity of other selves and other minds, so for Paul, who speaks as a theologian and who has already confirmed this *universal* longing of men, there is only *one* way: "Where the Spirit of the Lord is, there is freedom" (2 Cor. 3:17). This freedom is single and precise; it is "the freedom wherewith Christ has made us free" (Gal. 4:31). He knew that Christ had said two things: (1) "The Truth will set you free," and (2) "*I* am the Truth, the Way, and the Life."

II

So much, then, for an introduction and for an attempt at suggesting the location of the true problem of freedom. The task which now lies before us is to examine at closer quarters and in more concrete fashion the relation between freedom, an infinite, and limitation or Law, a finite, as these two things are mysteriously located in an identity of action and being. By way of trying to accomplish this fairly thorny objective, let us look at this identity as it emerges (or is neglected) in the following situations, all analogous to one another:

(1) The interior structure and action of the individual human personality,

(2) The education of the human person,

(3) The person versus technology,

(4) The person and the total cosmos of finite reality, and let this series of four brief studies represent, however sketchily, the different levels of the lower and human analogies of freedom's mystery.

(5) We will conclude with an examination of the identity of Law and freedom as it is set forth in the theology of Saint Paul, and this will represent the mystery as it exists for man on the supernatural or divine level.

Our first hope is that the materials and situations of the lower, the natural order will illuminate those of the higher, the supernatural. But an even stronger hope is exactly the reverse of this, namely, that the startling and ecstatic structure of the relationship between Law and freedom as it exists on the final theological plane, between God the ultimate Law and man at his final point of freedom, will so illuminate the problems and materials of our lower, earthly situation that our Christian courage and assurance will be intensified for the quest of earthly liberty far beyond all secular dreams, energies, hopes, and courage. There is no call whatsoever that we play the role of second, and objecting, and cautious fiddle in this contemporary debate, in this contemporary thirst to be everywhere and as much as possible, free.

FREEDOM AND THE PERSONAL INTERIOR

Let us again take a simple glance at ourselves. Can we not see, with even a cursory inward glance, that there are two principles in us:

(a) First of all, there is the principle (or self) in us which can be exactly *measured,* felt and defined as being this thing or person and no other thing or person. What is the use of using technical language here? Everybody, intellectual or farmer, knows the sense of what we are talking about, and it can be reduced to the following: Whatever we are, whatever we are on the inside of us, this inside comes to an outside; that is, it has boundaries. Where we end we can say that another person begins. Everything in us is specific and unique, our own and no other's—the hair, the teeth, the heart, the feelings, the mind—everything. This is the narrow thing we have been talking about, which, when we have it, we have very little in the eyes of the world; so that "narrow," thus used, is a pejorative phrase. But if used properly, it is a thing which, when we possess it, means the having, the feeling, the possession of the self, the *unum necessarium,* the one thing necessary. On the level of human mystery, on the level, too, of ordinary human psychology, it means to have very little and yet to have very much. We can live on the surface of this self and think we possess it, and we can live, by an American or any other form of prestige, on the surface of endless other selves and think we possess them. But though this thing be narrow and limited, it is deep; it is a depth, and we must go endlessly down into it before we can truly possess either our own souls or, in charity, the souls of others . . . but the important point for the moment is that we are *only* ourselves and not everything else.

The word "only" is the beginning of the problem. For the word means bounded, limited, contained, determined to be one thing, and therefore not free. As a restricting and restricted thing, this being only oneself, is our first form of Law. And if, whether they believe in Him or not, men can imagine God making this self, they should imagine Him as first thinking of it, and then making, and equivalently saying to it: be *this*. If we wish to imagine further and truly, we should conceive of Him as issuing a command: do *this*—a phrase by which I mean simply to suggest a divine command to us to take up and accept ourselves with an act of the will, not pretending that we can stand, as it were, conveniently outside of ourselves as though we were angelic intelligences surveying the problem of ourselves from a convenient distance. God has specified us down to the level of the "only," we are not free, we are our specific selves, and this is the first and most fundamental and bothersome example of Law, which is always a finite. There is a phrase which is used in an unfortunate sense by many, but which also has a fortunate sense, if taken according to the spirit of our analysis. It is: *Let us be a Law* unto ourselves.

(b) On the other hand, there is a second principle in us which is in some way the exact antithesis of this first highly limited principle. It is that which we call freedom. Of it we might give many technical definitions. But let it be enough first to say again that it is something in us which wishes to be without bounds. We are in pain if we feel restraint. We are only happy if we feel that we are without it. There is some incredible will in us not to be something but to be everything. Here it is difficult to speak correctly and perhaps the existence and final validity, the complete goodness of this wish, will only be able to be understood and acknowledged at the close of this essay, when we will see that, corresponding to the natural drive toward complete freedom, and, therefore, toward a kind of divinization of ourselves, there is actually a supernatural Christian mystery according to which this impulsion is not only recognized, but accomplished. Let us only say now that this second principle, this will to be so free, to be without limitation (and, let us say it, without Law) is really in us, and that, on the surface, it seems to be a lawless principle.

But to come to this last conclusion would be a begging of our whole question, a coming to a too rapid conclusion. There is not only a bad, there is also a good thirst in us to be without Law, and we solve nothing by ignoring this *fact*. Nor did St. Paul ignore or evade it; indeed, he proclaimed the pre-eminence of liberty. But is not the whole and the true question the relationship between freedom and the Law, the infinite and the finite in us? Is not the whole question whether we become free—that is to say, lawless—by lawlessness or by passage through the Law, by escape or by a highly actual movement of the principle of freedom through the principle of non-freedom in us? In the concrete this means: shall we, in order to be free and get free, choose to walk through the reality of our own selves and our own lives, or shall we choose to try to create some other specious world in which to live and walk outside of ourselves, and, therefore, outside of reality?

Actually, there never has been any other path to liberty. There never has been any other kind of human self save a narrow (though deep) one. How could there be? What Christianity has done is to project this truth into clearer focus, intensify it, and reject attempts to escape it through various externalisms and immediate infinities. Finally, it has presented to the world newer and higher levels on which the structure of this identity between Law and freedom, the restricted and the unrestricted, not only remains true, but more highly true. I think here once more of the situation of the coming of Christ. The Jews before Him had, of course, been given bodies and narrow selves, and it was perfectly right and proper (indeed, it was a divine ordinance) that there should proceed from the small self and heart the offering of external sacrifice. But if the latter did not proceed truly from the inward heart, becoming shall we say, the heart written out in larger letters, it could (and actually did) pass into pure externalism, a flight from the true passage into God and freedom. It was at this moment that Christ entered into the world to intensify this passage in both an old and a new way. Those first words of His in the womb keep haunting the mind. "Sacrifices and oblations Thou wouldst not. But a body hast Thou fitted unto me. . . . And then I said: behold I come." This "behold I come" is nothing more than the rush of freedom into the body and the self in order to accomplish freedom, to reach it. And in our own lesser way we duplicate this Christic act whenever the one principle in us (freedom) enters as totally as possible with acceptance and embrace into the other principle in us (the restricted, the bound, the "only"). So we may conceive that in this text Christ is really saying two things: First of all, He says "behold I come" as an address to His body; secondly, He says it as an address to His Father (the free one and the free thing par excellence) toward whom he thus sets himself on the march.

We are at last forced toward that question which is very difficult indeed to answer. How is it possible that the narrow and the finite principle (or the Law), being entered into by freedom, not only does not destroy freedom but even realizes or creates it? This is certainly a difficult question, but the real contemporary difficulty about it almost as certainly comes from the way in which the question is put and the kind of answer to it which seems to be expected. As Mr. Fergusson points out in his commentary on *The Divine Comedy*, the question is put by the "rational" mind expecting a "rational" answer in terms of the brilliant but surface intelligence. Such a mind is always thinking "univocally" in terms of either-or. It is speaking in the following terms to itself. Either a human action must be free or it must be limited; but how can it be free if it is completely seized, to its very innards, by the limited, by Law?

In such terms, in terms of the pure and logical intelligence, there is probably no final answer. Only the doing, only the actual entering into the narrow real, will flood the whole intelligence, the whole being of man, with the light that two such disparate things can come together in one embrace. That which is taken so often as the only form of the intelligence, the logical reason, can maintain its spurious and departmentalized freedom outside of reality forever and think that by so doing it is creating the free *man*. But only in action, in the real taking up of the first principle (of limit, of Law) by the second principle (of boundlessness, of freedom) can the second really see itself in this moment as really born and changed from a purely speculative possibility to an order of fact.

FREEDOM AND EDUCATION

This, then, is the first and fundamental situation which illuminates the relation between Law and freedom, a situation which exists at the very interior of each man. The reason why Law is considered an enemy of or a block to freedom is that it is seen as something altogether exterior to the latter and imposing itself by force and from the outside upon the latter. In this first instance we have seen that this is not so at all, that the first Law is nothing but the self, and that between it and its freedom there is (or can and should be!) a relation of complete interiority. Law or legislation written in codes, when it is good law, is nothing more than a series of formulas which commands a man to do what is for his own good. Also, it does nothing more than command him to be free.

Let us pass on now to our second analogue of this relationship between the two principles. I am thinking of the whole problem of the education of the human soul, and specifically of the relationship between the teacher and student. Let us look upon the teacher as a form of the Law and upon the student as a form of free being, possessing, or capable of possessing the inward freedom which we have described in our first section. The critical question is: Shall he, the teacher, the Law, impose himself, his views, his knowledge, from the outside, as one who is exterior to freedom, restraining it, compelling it? Or shall he, somehow or other, become interior to this other self before him, in some way or other identical with him, and thus helping us again to break down the relation of exteriority between freedom and Law? Let us describe the concrete and ideal situation of the classroom (or, for that matter, of any other relationship which we can call educational) in the following way. Two human beings confront each other. One of them is equipped with a set of real experiences and a rational, critical gift which explains and unites these experiences. He knows this, but he also knows that he himself can still grow beyond his present moment of experience, knowledge and power of theoretical and practical conclusion. Before him is another human being, in embryo and beginning, so far as the substance of all these things is concerned. Let us suppose that, in terms of actual knowledge, he knows very little, but that he can grow endlessly, if not prevented from the outside. Actually, he needs the outside, the teacher, but the teacher must penetrate, his knowledge must enter in, in such a way that he does not impose himself; in such a way that the student remains himself, and is himself discovering the truth. Ideally, then, the teacher will relive his thinking before the student, and the latter will relive it as his own and freely (though it would be good if the teacher should not totally relive the content of his intelligence at any moment but so limit himself—O terrible pedagogical discipline—to only the basic rhythms of the problem that the student can himself complete the rhythm and perhaps—tragic pedagogical moment—pass some day in insight beyond the teacher). If therefore, the teacher does enter as a form of Law, the entrance must at each step be recognized by the receiver as his own living, not that of an outsider's; it must be a living which he passes through with spontaneity and freedom. Only where this happens does the externality and the pressure of the Law vanish, and only so does it join in another and second profound relationship with freedom.

Here let me suggest three illustrious delineations of this process, as they are drawn from three of its great masters in the history of the West. They are Aeschylus, the tragedian, Socrates, the philosopher, and St. Ignatius of Loyola, a master of the Christian spiritual life. The work of all three bears directly on the educational relation of Law and freedom, teacher and student.

(a) We begin with the *Suppliants* of Aeschylus, and here I acknowledge my debt to the brief commentary on this play by Eric Voegelin in his *The New Science of Politics*.

In the *Suppliants,* Pelasgus, the king of Argos, is presented, as a ruler, with an excruciating problem through which he must live and come to a conclusion. Shall he give up the suppliants to the Egyptians, or, for not having given them over, cause the sending of his people to war with the Egyptians? Having suffered through to the climax of an action taken by himself—and this is suffering, this naked descent of the soul into itself to discover in agony the ground and direction of right action—his second task is so to present to his people the totality of this experience as ruler that they will relive it and inwardly consent to his conclusions—to the point where, *both* freely and in communion with him, they take up the consequences of war upon themselves.

(b) The next example of that method of teaching which so unites the teacher and the student that Law and freedom enter into an intimate relationship of identity is Socrates or Socrates-Plato. The method is called *maieutica* or midwifery by Socrates and is closely associated with the whole Socratic-Platonic metaphysics of the Theory of Ideas and the doctrine of Recollection. Certainly these are all large and technical terms, but for our purposes they can be reduced to a simplicity which will not do violence to all their refinements and subtleties.

There is, I think Socrates would say, a deep form and content of knowledge which is already present in the human soul before anybody touches it by any kind of pedagogical communication from the outside. He uses a highly imaginative myth which he calls the myth of Recollection and a metaphysics whose core he calls the Ideas to explain this content in the soul which must be stimulated into conscious life by the teacher. According to the way in which he presents the meaning of Recollection (though I am convinced that he is deliberately putting solid truths of the psyche into this strange, mythical form), we must think of the soul as having passed through previous existences in which it was in conscious, visional contact with all the great central and model ideas of reality. And the function of the teacher would be, adroitly and sympathetically, by question rather than through the imposed forms of a new external knowledge, to revive these memories which already exist within the soul. So that the Law which comes from without and which could have come in the form of imposing declarations now comes in the form of a method which helps the soul freely to discover itself. Thus all knowledge which comes from the outside is friendly because it is already inside; the learning soul, therefore, does not meet an invader but rather itself, and has not been imposed upon or compelled.

I hope it is unnecessary to insert apologies here for certain qualities in this Socratic picture of learning, or to explain away certain of its apparent crudities. For it would be out of place to distract the reader with any gesture toward a careful and elaborated theory of knowledge. Let me simply point out, by way of acknowledging the fundamentally sound instinct behind this Socratic theorizing, that even St. Thomas himself did not hesitate to say: *Anima est quodammodo omnia,* the soul is in some sense everything. And surely there must be a sense in which the soul, as it takes knowledge after knowledge into itself, must already (or at least potentially) be these things it comes to know; or how else could it come to recognize them?

But, after all, we are not now talking about technical theories of knowledge as such. We are only trying to create, by direction and indirection, some true feeling for that sensitive situation which the teacher must face when he confronts the abyss of freedom and potentiality represented by the student soul before him. This latter thing is an infinite, though it takes the first form of a seed in embryonic helplessness, moving forward under the impulsion of an ouside pedagogical Law. The teacher can make either one of two fundamental errors. He can impel in such a way that he compels, and removes the sense of freedom from this glorious flight and adventure of so always brilliant a seed. Or he can produce the same unfortunate effect by imposing his own limitations upon it, with a kind of thus-far-and-no-further attitude; as if his own present and sometimes immobilized intellectual and spiritual state of the moment, instead of acting as a modest point of passage, a concrete but not final point of Law, should pose operationally as the eternal Law itself.

There is one sentence in the psalms which describes this mystery of the movement of the soul and its freedom, in or out of the classroom: "As the hart panteth after the fountain of water, so does my soul pant after Thee, O my God." In front of such a mystery, the teacher must surely wish to become an extraordinary mixture of active impulsion and passive forbearance, knowing what is his task and what is none of his business, entering in but not taking over, touching the free center, yet leaving the center untouched—because it is the *secret of the King.*

(c) It is at this point that I should like to introduce some passages from the *Spiritual Exercises* of St. Ignatius which are a third completely relevant and even better analogue for the whole question of how to teach and be a Law to someone, and how at the same time to leave him free in the very act of contact with the Law.

The situation of St. Ignatius was this: He had himself passed through a crucial and overwhelming set of spiritual experiences which had brought him to the very height of the Christian spiritual life. In the document which we now call the *Spiritual Exercises,* he had systematically outlined the method by which the soul might repeat the passage he had taken and thus arrive at an eminent degree in the knowledge and the service of God. This method, in its very essence, is a detailed and concrete passage, by the meditating mind and all the sensibilities of man, through all the phases of the life of Christ, then through His resurrection and through His ascent back into His glorified and eternal life with the Father.

Now Ignatius himself had, contemplatively and actually, lived these mysteries according to that perfect mode of living and experiencing which we call sanctity. But clearly they could be relived by others according to many modes and many degrees of achieving and consent. One of his major problems in the composition of this famous document was so to instruct future directors of the *Exercises* that they would do two things: (1) They would indeed communicate to the soul of the exercitant all these lofty Christic materials to be relived by him. (2) They would do so in such a way, however, that they would not impose assent upon that soul. The center of the latter, its final point of freedom and contact with God, must remain uncompelled by the *Exercises,* even though the contact is effected by the *Exercises.* Therefore, listen to him say to the director:

He who gives to another the method and order of a meditation or contemplation ought faithfully to narrate the history of the contemplation or meditation, going through the points however only briefly, and with a short explanation: because when the person who contemplates takes the true groundwork of the history, discussing and reasoning by himself, and meeting with something that makes the history clearer and better felt (whether this happen through his own reasoning or through the enlightenment of his understanding by grace), he thereby enjoys greater spiritual relish and fruit than if he who gives the Exercises had minutely explained and developed the meaning of this history; for it is not to know much, but it is to understand and savor the matter interiorly that fills and satisfies he soul.

And listen again to him saying in the same spirit:

He who gives the exercises must not incline him who receives them more to poverty or to a vow than to their contraries, nor to one state or manner of life than to another; for although outside the Exercises we may lawfully and meritoriously induce all who are in all probability fitted for it to choose a life of continency, of virginity, a life in religion, or any kind of

evangelical perfection, nevertheless, during the time of the
Spiritual Exercises, when the soul is seeking the Divine will, it
is better and more fitting that its Creator and Lord Himself
communicate with the devout soul, inflaming it to love and
praise Him, and disposing it for that way of life by which it
will best serve him for the future; so that he who gives the
Exercises must himself not be influenced or inclined to one
side or another, but keeping as it were in equilibrium like a
balance, allow the Creator to act immediately with the creature,
and the creature with its Creator and Lord.

Of course Ignatius is here talking of the creating of a very
special relationship between the soul and God, but surely
the teacher is concerned with the creation of as special and
as free a relationship between the soul and the truth, so that
we can in general say the following: Behind these materials
from such diverse "pedagogical" masters in the Western tradition lies, certainly not a set of specifications for the conduct of a classroom or any teacher-student relation—that
would be an absurd pretension for these pages—but rather
a general pedagogical spirituality. This "spirituality" would
involve a number of mutually helpful attitudes on the part
of two so intimately related souls. The teacher would work
at, but refuse the temptation of controlling the student. He
would recognize that there is a core of sheer creativity in
the latter which can be fed but can never be predicted too
early by himself as to its form or its range. Creativity is an
extraordinary thing in the human soul, and it seems safe to
say that it is powerfully present in all of us. It is identical
with freedom, being blocked wherever that does not exist,
and it is identical with love. For given a chance, that is to
say, when it is not impeded by a purely external concept of
Law, there is something in us which shoots on and forward
with pure spontaneity, rejoicing in the discovery of the co-

realities of itself and the world. Under these circumstances, not only education but life itself becomes a constant adventure and a great joy. The student becomes aware of the teacher as a completely liberating Law, in that holy sense of "liberating" which is in a mysterious way caught up in the very interior of the narrowness of the Law and which we shall only adequately understand and accept when we see how it is echoed with joy by St. Paul on the very highest theological level of the understanding.

FREEDOM AND TECHNOLOGY

The teacher, then, can, as a form of Law, be either a block to freedom or a source, a concrete, limited but not limiting source of liberty and boundless creativity. It is up to him to decide, in the secret of his own heart and according to the degree of consciousness he has of this delicate problem, which he shall be. Nor is the student absolved of responsibility in this relationship, for he can degrade the most effective and creative forms of Law or limit if he chooses at heart to lead the life of a slave rather than that of a son of God. On the one hand, the teacher can become a limiting pressure, a Law in the most aboriginal sense of the term; on the other hand, the student can choose the teacher as an absolute image of himself for the sake of a very dubious safety, and thereby use the whole idea of limit not as a way, but as an end.

But now let us suppose, as is in very truth the case, that such a degradation of this Freedom-Law relation is endlessly multiplied throughout a whole society. We have decided that wherever there is restraint of liberty there is pain. And we have seen that wherever there is a corruption of the true

pedagogical situation, very unfortunate consequences can follow. The frightening question now leaps to the mind: What
are the terrible consequences in terms of spiritual pain if
everybody and everything in society tends to become a corrupt pedagogical Law and if I, on my part, am subtly con-
spiring to accept and even create this kind of total situation?
In the discussion that follows, there is no slightest intention
of devaluating technology as such, but only of stressing,
within the lines of our general argument, that this is one of
the greatest problems inherent in a technological world.

I hope it is accurate enough to say that such a world has
an ideal function, and that, if it restricts itself to the latter,
all will be well. That function is neither more nor less than
to supply endless forms of efficiency, ease, well-being, and
communication for the surfaces of human personalities—
and where we use the word "surface" we do not mean superficial. Though this last word is correctly used wherever technology pretends to create and dominate the total soul, dominating it by external pressures, creating it by saying that it
is competent to make man as such. Where it sticks to its last
as one among manifold forms of Law, it is indeed a magnificent structure and, on its own level, a guide to freedom.

It is perfectly true that our superb American technical
achievement *tells* us what we are to be and makes a social
world of other persons who, by duplicating ourselves exactly,
again tells us what to be, on the level of identical clothing,
modes of transportation, cleaning of teeth, writing of letters,
and on and on *ad infinitum*. These are indeed so many
forms of necessity forced upon us; but where these necessities
are truly helpful and their surface vocation is recognized
with clarity by the soul, it is only a profound lack of common sense that will reject them or not see their liberating
qualities. The real trouble and crisis begin when the repeti-

tive and the pressuring forms of the technical invade the deeper levels of the soul, relentlessly dictating to us the forms of our musical feeling, family life, patterns of friendship, art images, folklore, and education—to the point where it poses as a new Gospel, a new Christianity. And since all this is not within its competence, since it can only enter these depths as an incompetent stranger who cannot make these parts of man echo with the joy of the recognition of self or of the moving on toward deeper freedoms, it can only produce several tragic results. It will cause a great anger in the soul because of the presence of a restraining stranger in its most inward rooms. There will be deep resentment at the presence of a machine posing as Christ in the regions of the secret of the king—in the regions where the ideally free soul is finally become citizen of that Jerusalem which is free. That is because our age is not yet an age of spiritual freedom. Certainly we have admitted that this is a great age of freedom, and of a passion for it; but so far it is only a generation of political and social democracy protesting against political and social masters. And surely the profoundest instincts in us, if we will only be brave enough to know them, must tell us that these democracies, these freedoms, will turn into collapsible façades if they are not supported by even more important abysses of liberty.

We have said that technology is a magnificent achievement of the human spirit, one which very much belongs to the ascent of the soul to freedom and to God. About that fact there need be neither discussion nor argument. But it is so giantlike and so fascinating in its achievement that we have seen the danger of its becoming the single Law of men's lives and of drawing up all the nether regions of their souls to an identification with that surface level which is the preoccupation of the technical. In becoming this and doing this, it would indeed parody the words of Christ: "If I be lifted, I shall draw all things to Me."

There is only one kind of civilization which will be safe from this kind of domination by technology as a single law; it will be a civilization which is profoundly *pluralistic*. Let me explain what is meant by this word in this context.

I mean that whenever a great technical achievement is created, we can only both rightly use it and be safe from it if there exist by its side other equally powerful reality-structures which are so marvellously in tune with the souls of men and of such an affinity with their various depths that by their very existence and attracting power they prevent a single and technical law from operating in society. The matter might be put this way: The human personality is articulated into many levels of being, many planes of energy which differ in quality and importance. For the fulfillment of each of these in freedom, there is the necessity, in a really mature civilization, of a corresponding external reality-structure to serve as Law, as a carefully defined path for its liberty or its liberation. Technology will allow a part of man to enter into a friendly and liberating relation with the necessities of matter. A first-rate and truly qualitative victory in the arts will lead vast areas of man toward expression and freedom, and will prevent these areas from dying under the weight of cheap, sentimental and surface creation by the entertainment engineers of great corporations. The state, or political society, will liberate the community instincts of men toward that point where they enter into common action in freedom and love (because legislation is made acceptable to men after the manner we have depicted between the King of Argos and his people). The relation of the Church to the profoundest depths of the soul is so vast a subject that we can only mention it here and pass on in modesty.

FREEDOM AND REALITY

We now come to the last, the largest, the most all-inclusive finite situation in which the human person expresses his freedom by the very act of his contact with Law. I refer to the contact of the soul, not with any particular version of finite reality or of its limiting laws, whether it be with the self, the teacher, the lawgiver, the technocrat, or anything else, but with nothing less than the whole of finite reality under God as it is encountered in a particular lifetime.

How many questions could we not raise about this final confrontation of human freedom with this final form of reality and Law before it reaches God. But wisdom suggests that we limit ourselves to crucial questions; and so, out of all the possible forms of the latter, I elect one which seems to be crucial indeed: the question whether the attitude of our freedom toward all that we shall meet in this life is one of the necessity of complete control or of a recognition that such control is impossible. This is a pre-eminent matter for men to determine, and thereon, as we shall see, hangs the whole tale of Christianity. On the decision between these two attitudes depends also the ultimate success or failure of freedom as it tries to achieve itself in the inner embrace of the limited.

We can admit and have admitted that freedom is only reached and made by walking in and through a definite world. Every other form of liberty is completely fraudulent because it is a non-existent dream and represents a flight into the freedom of a dream world. But does the walk through *this* lifetime, *this* portion of human history, *these* people, *this* death, *this* possible bomb, mean that true freedom must control these things in absoluteness or not be free? It does not. What in fact I wish to suggest is the very reverse, that such an absolute passion for the mastery of the finite means the end of freedom for either society or the soul, or for both. Let us examine this suggestion.

(1) *Absolute control of finite reality is the end of freedom for society:* because the pretension of such a "closed" society is to have come to a point where it is capable of saying: We have a system which is foolproof against collapse; we have a leader in whom we can place complete trust and from whom we gather the sense of divine paternity; we have a constitution which will make us inviolate against every danger to political freedom, and this without any further thinking or living on our part. In a word, we have constructed some inviolable point of security. . . . Now what else is all this but to protect ourselves, speciously and fraudulently, against any further invasions, beyond such frontiers, by further finite realities or by God Himself? We become closed off against the relentless movements of reality, and like children we keep saying (through the instruments we have named): A new reality is coming in the next moment of history, a new danger, but there is nothing new, there is no danger, there dare not be, because Big Brother (*1984*) is near. If, therefore, the free society is the open society, ruled indeed by order but not by one of the great mystiques of the modern world (such as the communist or fascist leader), if the free society is not bound like a slave to any absolute, fixed point, then the absolute control of reality is a form, not of liberty, but of slavery. To be able to predict and anticipate every eventuality is not freedom. Actually this control is impossible, but the point is that, in our passion for safety over against liberty, we pretend that it is altogether possible. And in so doing, instead of making Law a way in freedom, we make it a counterfeit of the face of the Living God and of the heavenly Jerusalem. Instead of progressively vanishing as Law through

its interiority and its acceptability to men, the Law becomes completely fixed, external, and hateful, crushing the bodies and souls of men.

(2) If this is true of human society, how much more does it hold for the individual if he insists, by way of eliminating fear, that reality can be so controlled. He spends all his energies, night and day, in planning that no unplanned reality, whether in the form of men or God, shall enter in upon him. And thus he refuses and destroys the smooth, spontaneous path to freedom which is below all thought and calculation, he is afraid of the open, interior dictates of the Holy Spirit, which is indeed the spirit of Law but which, asking for no eternal pause in any Law, seeks a constant moving on toward the city of freedom.

Let us stop again to summarize what we have been saying: Law is a beautiful thing, the way to freedom, the way which, if fully entered into with love, vanishes as law. The passage through it, through all the finite structures of the human, together with all the full decisions and complete commitments this passage involves, is the existential path to liberty. So that, unlike many Protestant theories, ours does not have to hold off from an uninhibited entrance into the finite by the specious invention of a "transcendent self" which always keeps itself unspotted from the real, concrete everyday self of human history. Nevertheless, our commitment, unhesitating and never partial though it may be, does not mean rigidity or slavery.

Two forms of the latter are, on the level of the person, neurosis, and, on the level of the social group, the ideological idea or program. Neurosis is basically a Manichaean distrust of, or failure to grasp, the profound worthwhileness of the fundamental abyss of being that is the human self—below all absolute indentifications of the self with precise categories.

A neurotic age loses this contact with being, and in counter-action establishes all sorts of rigid and absolute defenses in the soul, defenses which must be held at any cost against the entrance of reality into unworthy depths. In society an ideology does the same thing. Like the soul itself, human history is a brilliant, efflorating process, pushing man toward a freedom and total consciousness that can only be consummated in God. But the ideologist selects a single, narrow form—let it be race, class, big business, big labor, big agriculture, a political party, a single politician, a man on a white horse—and imposes it, as a restricting, totally defining force, on the whole of this rich pluralistic reality.

As I write these last lines, the thought occurs to me that in these our days our principal fear is perhaps not at all the fear of Law. If indeed we were faithful to the latter in all its forms, we would be being faithful to nothing less than reality itself in all its forms. And it seems safe to say that there is not only a drive in the human person which, in the very act of his fidelity to particular reality-situations, impels him on and on with a growing thirst for the real, no matter what it may hold —but also that there is also the same kind of forward movement in reality itself which is asking for commitment but forbidding idolatry. Thus also, a real Law certainly asks for commitment, for veneration, for entrance into its narrow self by the whole human self; it knows it can be defined according to clear, unmistakable language and principle; but it does not pretend to define the whole of reality. It says in all realism: I have brothers and sisters; I am not the Lord thy God. I will help to create freedom in you, but will not in the doing take it away from you; you are afraid of an open and undefined reality that cannot be reduced to the single thought of some single mind; you do not want the Christian adventure, within the terms of which the real can only be "controlled" by a Faith, a Hope, and a Charity rooted in the Living God alone. You do not want a real order in your life, an order which is built laboriously by complicated *thought* and the athletic relating of many diversified forms of human *feeling*, instead of being built on one thought or one feeling. You wish even me, when I take the form of some one fixed law (e.g., "Thou shalt love thy neighbor") to be fixed in the sense of being closed to all further thought, effort, or adaptation to situation (for St. Thomas himself would surely have said that we must love our neighbor not in some obnoxious, univocal, unchanging sense, but shiftingly, proportionately, according as my neighbor is mother, father, brother, sister, friend, enemy, fellow citizen, sick or well, in the heat of the working sun, in the contemplative cool of the evening); it is true that I as a law fix everything that relates to me, but I cannot and will not do for you what mothers are expected to do for those who are still children, namely, determine the future and explain every possible variation of myself which you will meet. In a word, I determine everything and I determine nothing. I do two things: I command you to follow me (as a nest of freedom), but I cannot tell you what will be the next form of myself, what the proportion, what analogical mode of being I will take; you deceive yourself by thinking that if you can close reality and the future, if you can make it simple, controlled, and altogether determined, you will remove all fear; you think that you can invent some counterfeit of true love, some all-covering mystique in the order of politics which will give you physical safety, or some single generalization which will give you emotional security, or some simple, well-defined formula which will stop the movement of your soul to God within limits you will yourself define. But in reality both these closed souls and these closed states are houses of fear, and they are not free.

FREEDOM AND LAW IN ST. PAUL

Perhaps we are now in a better position to look at the relationship between freedom and Law as it exists on the purest level of theology. Certainly if all that we have been saying of this relationship on its human planes is also true on this final plane of being, if God himself has declared that in the very act of keeping the Law the soul becomes so free that it is as though there were no law, then our discussion will indeed have reached a happy climax. It will certainly fortify our conviction that human freedom is to be achieved only by embracing the definite, the limiting, the Law. But this is one of the major messages of the theology of St. Paul.

It is perfectly obvious in Paul's theorizing about Law that with the appearance of Christ the Christian has been freed from the intolerable weight of the infinitely detailed prescriptions of the Mosaic Law, and that this has meant the lifting of an intolerable burden from the human spirit. But the question we are pursuing is much larger in significance than this. What St. Paul is saying (and here I follow the brilliant discussion of Father Stanislas Lyonnet, S.J., in his "Liberté Chrétienne et Loi de l'Esprit," *Christus,* October, 1954, pp. 6–27) is that the weight of every law as Law has been lifted from that spirit. And this means even the burden, as burden, of the Ten Commandments as commandments. Though, of course, it does not at all mean that the content of this good life has been changed for, or can be changed by, the Christian. It means something far higher than this. It means that, where once there was nothing but the spirit of slavery and externality before the Law, now there remains nothing but freedom and interiority. Nor by freedom do we mean freedom from the Law, but freedom in it; as by interiority we do not mean that Protestant form of unmediated interiority by which the soul leaps over all reality and Law to face God directly, but rather that inwardness by which the demands of finite reality are seen to be in basic rhythmic tune with the deepest, most spontaneous desires of man and by which man, at his most central point, is impelled toward reality through the inward, driving presence of the Holy Spirit, a Spirit which moves us not by the power of "decision-making" in the face of things alien to our nature, but exclusively by the fires of "wanting," of "wishing, of holy desire, and of love." Decision and the burden of it, God knows, are necessary; but they are fraught with pain, with abandonment of one good for another (and who really wishes to give up anything?), with all kinds of struggles which take place on the upper surfaces of the will as it "battles" reality (and who really wishes to battle, who does not wish to rest?). As long as we are merely "deciding" we have not yet entered into these roots of the soul to which belong the more effortless regions of love and spontaneity and freedom. Decisions are, to be sure, a necessary prelude to wanting and to love. But they do not partake of the final free nature of either.

Even in his fundamental Christology, Paul is aware of this. His awareness is particularly projected in his pictures of the beginning and the end of Christ's life. The beginning: for Christ does not take on a body because He has merely decided; He takes it on because He wishes to, fully, brilliantly ("And then I said, Behold I come"). And He dies, not by an arbitrary decision of election between living and dying, but because he wishes to (*oblatus est quia voluit*, "he was offered up because he wanted to"). "With desire have I desired to eat this Pasch with you."

For Paul the life of grace is the life of freedom, over against the Old Testament of Law. Under grace a man does not obey the Law out of a spirit of necessity, which would make all law doubly Law, but out of an inward groaning and desire of the Holy Ghost for very love of reality. For all reality, but especially for homely, concrete reality, the world of the real God of Abraham, Isaac, and Jacob.

Therefore, Paul can say to the Christian: You are no longer under the Law, but under grace (Rom. 6, 14). Father Lyonnet particularly invokes St. Thomas' analysis of Pauline thought on the subject of freedom and law. St. Thomas tells us that the New Law is the Law of the Spirit, and that this Law is actually indentical with the person and the activity of the Holy Spirit dwelling in us. "It is the Holy Spirit himself which is the New Testament producing in us love, the plenitude of the Law." So that, again in the words of Father Lyonnet, the Law is now both a free act of man and an act of God Himself, of that Holy Spirit who operates in us. It is He who, according to the wonderful expression of Cardinal Serapando, has been received by the Christian in the guise of Law.

Finally, what happens to the externality of the Law? An amazing thing which brings us to the very height and depth of the new, ontological mysteries of Christianity. We know that, according to St. Paul and his greatest commentators, the Law, as a simple external norm of conduct, does not vivify, but that actually "the letter [any merely external law] killeth." We know in addition (a fact which sums up the whole point of this essay) that the new Law was not born on the day of promulgation of the details of the Sermon on the Mount, but on the Day of Pentecost, when the Law was inscribed in the hearts of men. Now the question is, What then happens to the external Law?

In a sense, nothing in it has changed. In another sense, all has changed. For even in its external mode it becomes centered not so much in a set of legislative formulas or deducible principles as in the person of Christ, who contains and is all these things. To do the things which Christ did or would do is the whole Law. To do them out of love of Him, the Only

Begotten Son of God, becomes the sole motivation of the Law. Thus all ancient externalisms now have melted into His person, and He has entered into us to become one with us, so that the love of self, the love of all men, the love of God are all comprised in the love of Him with Whom we have become mystically but truly identical; so that we have at last become one with the Law, not only in a unity of love, but in a profound ontological unity of fact. Here at the ultimate point of Law we embrace in the one act the finite humanity of Christ and the Infinite God, the limit and the unlimited, law and freedom. There is no other name in heaven or on earth in which the difference between these things, the painful differences, completely vanish.

And if we, in the mystery of the Church, are Christ, and in Him divinized, then is the Law altogether dead. We are no longer exterior strangers, but citizens already of that heaven which is free.

5

CULTURE AND BELIEF

This is an experimental and tentative analysis of the relations existing between the twin problems of culture and belief. There never was a time when the possibility of belief was a more exacerbating problem for the intellectual who has not yet succeeded in reaching belief; but the same difficulties exist, and with equal intensity, for the phenomena of culture and society. Where is there validity in entering into them for the alientated individual? Are there any possibilities of sincerity in doing so? I do not intend to examine such questions directly. All I propose is an analysis of epistemological method, throughout which it will be suggested that belief has a tendency to become difficult without some kind of commitment to a culture, some kind of belonging. If this is so, then the problem and the failure of faith must be assessed differently in different periods of history, and little comfort would remain for the believer who, by his various retreats from existence, is himself partly responsible for the decadence and collapse of a culture.

Nevertheless, the intellectual, while he may not enter into the world of guilt, may at least add to the danger of the situa-

tion if he begins to enjoy the subtle pleasures of his alienation from society, if he begins to elevate the tragic *incident*
of his isolation into a *metaphysical* value and to propose that
the isolated intelligence is the finest epistemological instrument for bringing judgment on either society or belief.

I

It is true that the quality of self-consciousness and liberty
and the drive toward the knowledge and possession of self-
hood are perhaps deeper in our day than in any other epoch.
Neither is there any doubt that the cosmic sense is there; it
has had its effect in causing great upheavals in our human
situation and in deepening the sense of the human person.
And the quality of modern sensibility, all the way from the
private sensibility of the artist to that of the political drive
toward democracy, is, to put it mildly, an extraordinary
thing. But the phenomenon we have first had to deal with is
the necessary moment of complete alienation between our
two polarities, between the person and society history-cosmos-
God. Every symptom we could detect has been painfully and
paradoxically at odds with the magnificent polarities, wedded,
conjoined, of a St. Augustine. The human problems we have
had on our hands, and substantially still have, are: the difficulty of the insertion of this intellectual into any social or
cosmic order and the difficulty for him of belief. It is not
enough to attack the individual for his failures in these directions; there is also the matter of an atmosphere in which
he is forced to live. This atmosphere of isolation and alienation, of the radical separation of our two polarities, may be
summarized under the following brief headings:
1. There never was a time when the mind was more affected by the terrible remoteness of God. For many He has

never seemed less immanent. The sense of an underlying nothing is not the dream of Heidegger. The latter's work is the symptom of a common disease. Nor is this sense of nothingness Dionysian or Nietzschean in size. It is flat, empty, and, in this sense only, heroically appalling—an ironic counterpart of the clear, formed but corrupt world of daylight.

2. The alienation from the organism of society is still profound. This holds especially for the intellectual, who has often regarded society as his enemy. This loneliness and isolation from the community is general, and even the Catholic is being quite naive who thinks he is not being terribly affected by the same. As we have seen earlier in these pages, democracy at the moment is too often a deceptive imitation of a true community. Actually it is afraid of the insertion of true departmental or pluralistic societies into its own structure. It considers such insertions as an *invasion* of that political life which at best is an assurance that every man can live his own life and be disturbed by no one. Actual society becomes more and more a levelling and abstractionist process, and the hard realities of individual sensibility are thrust off in a corner to be saved or perish as they will. We have also, of course, become suspicious of *statism;* but we have identified state and society and the result is a meta-physical concept of community which takes on all the suspicious qualities of statism. For many intellectuals, to enter a society means a failure of nerve.

3. As for the sense of history, we were never more conscious of the immanent and open drive of the historical. But at the very moment when the impulse and the shock of history were thus impinging on the consciousness, we were suffering and are still suffering from a historical rootlessness that has little sympathy with tradition or evolution and could, therefore, be the seed-ground for the most violent kind of revolution. The

idea of the Waste Land came easily to be accepted as the symbol of our historical isolation.

Actually, in our day there is an unprecedented growth of interiority through an epochal development of the sense of society, cosmos, history. But *now*, at this moment, it just as important to note that in the case of these two worlds, interior and exterior, there is no clear penetration of one into the other. We are confronted by two worlds that simply do not harmonize.

We are at the end of the first great phase of the Copernican revolution, and the absoluteness, the breadth, the shock of it have been responsible for as much introversion as interiority. So, too, with the social and industrial revolutions. They are filled with so many undigested or false or inhuman forms that the sensitive individual often finds it impossible to insert himself into any order. The cosmology and society of Dante were human affairs, full of the analogies of the human, to which the deeper biological forces and instincts of man could react. And this was true, though in a far simpler fashion, of the Greek cosmos and the Greek citizen. The Homeric world was a "naive" world (I use this word in no pejorative sense). It was a cosmology which reflected the human, in which man could be at home with objects and could be fascinated by them in an objective way. On the other hand, Karl Jaspers (and many others, I am sure) has said that it is impossible for modern man to be naive. Man approaches the external as a *stranger,* with the mood of hostility. He is living through a deep crisis where introversion mingles with interiority. He finds he is faced with himself, a deep and infinitely complicated self, to a particularly cruel degree. Camus calls man by the formal title of *stranger* and he means that the cosmos is an enemy. And one need not comment on the example of the man of Kafka's parables, the prey of a monstrous universe that will not give up its secrets. There is no doubt that in all this we are dealing with the very reverse of the happy ideal of the "new concrete," where man would be organically "at home" in the universe and open, with all the supporting weight of this ever-growing body of his, to the infinite.

What is the epistemological danger in this situation? Actually, the double danger we are about to discuss has already been verified in fact, and it would be interesting and perhaps valuable to suggest a series of studies of modern literature that might produce an unhappy documentation of this fact.

1. First of all, there has been a whole series of what might be called narrow and unilinear attacks on single segments of reality, with the ambition of breaking through to "existence" and to some object of belief. This is an impossible epistemological method, for we cannot "break through" the surface of the real without engendering a corresponding series of repulsions that induce and will induce the sense of strangeness, impossibility and introversion. The second half of this chapter will suggest the nature of a more flexible epistemology which, to take but one example, will imitate the method of a Plato, who, as we have seen, knew how to circumambulate the introspective impossibilities of human nature, who allowed his mind to flow out into the analogies of society and the cosmos, and to return with ever-increasing understanding to the isolated darkness of man. It is, finally, rather by this kind of flexibility on the horizontal plane, this refusal to make an idol or fetish out of any one approach to the real, this more patient approach to existence, that the human intelligence can "break through." Our analysis will also fit these same thoughts into the doctrines of analogical realism and connaturality in the metaphysics of St. Thomas.

2. Secondly, there has been a general tendency to exalt the isolated, uninserted intelligence as the best instrument for the study of existence. But Dostoevski knew what he was talking about in saying that when a man leaves the people he becomes an athiest. And a phenomenologist like Scheler was convinced that, because of the eternal relation between charity and truth, it is impossible to find the truth outside the human community.

These, then, are the dangers and, indeed, the actualities. I abstain completely from the matter of guilt. For who is to say how difficult it is for men to be flexible and patient or to insert themselves in such a time as ours. The only purpose of this chapter is to examine the legitimacy and possibilities of different methods of search, and to try to highlight those directions where facility may lie.

1. UNILINEAR ATTACKS ON REALITY

Let me illustrate what is meant by an overnarrow, what might be called a vertical, attack on reality—an attempt literally to *penetrate* it. Some of the examples are admittedly extraordinary, others pathological, but I believe that, even where they are such, they are symbolic of more general and more normal tendencies in the same direction.

The insistent knocking at the door of the subconscious held for some the promise of producing amazing results in the order of poetic knowledge. The surrealist attempt to explore the "night" of self was a typical adventure of this kind; it was an attempt to build up a new *real* out of the resources of our own profounder sensibilities—to give sense to the day by exploring the night. Like existentialism itself, it could have been called a revolt against the surface, limited, contradictory forms of existence, against the "rhetoric" of life. As André Breton put it:

Everything suggests the belief that there is a certain point of the mind where life and death, the real and the imaginary, the past and the future, the communicable and the incommunicable, the high and the low are no longer perceived as contradictions. It would be vain to look for any motive in surrealist activity other than the hope of determining that point.

On which the comment of Marcel Raymond in his *From Baudelaire to Surrealism* was:

Possibly the surrealists as a whole, orthodox or not, have been lacking in patience. They have tried to force the unconscious, to conquer by violence secrets that might be revealed more readily to more artless minds.[1]

In a sense all of modern poetry is surrealist, so far as it is no longer merely ornamental or illustrative or entertaining but is now metaphysical in its ambitions, a voyage of discovery into existence, as much a source of knowledge as science itself. In some places, however, as in Rimbaud and Mallarmé, its desires have been absolute, its intention has been to construct an Absolute, *the* symbols, *the* metaphor, *the* Book that would give us the ultimate secret.

There is the same fundamentally hysterical state of soul that springs from the exploration into matter and the attempt to penetrate it at any cost. One is reminded of the scene from *Nausée* where the hero of Sartre picks up the root of a plant. He can reduce it to intelligibility to a degree; as a function it is conceptually penetrable; but the color, the rich muddiness, the *disgusting* and irrational effervescence of its particularity—these are things that make it, and the rest of

[1] *From Baudelaire to Surrealism.* By Marcel Raymond. New York: Wittenborn, Schultz, Inc., 1950.

the world with it, the enemy of the human intelligence. One is here in the presence of real frustration and despair. We are watching a strained, impatient and fantastic attempt to penetrate barriers in a straight line of attack. Such a spirit does not brook opposition and plunges forward even more desperately when it meets it. Indeed, Sartre's total description of the human thing offers a striking parallel to the above picture. For he describes human consciousness as essentially a divided, a fissured thing that is condemned to try endlessly *to reach a point of unity in itself,* to conquer temporarily, to found itself after the manner of God.

It is hard to say how many attempts have been made to discover or create some *one point* where value is to be found or reality discovered or salvation secured. For a good number it has been the point of liberty in human nature as the source of being and value. For others it has been sincerity. And there has been Gide's corruption of the concept of purity. With Valéry we have the effort to reduce self to a form of pure consciousness, and again I cite Raymond (because he hits off the present theme so perfectly):

At the end of this intellectual asceticism, the pure *self* tends to become a cosmic point, an anonymous power, without any individual support. Valéry bears witness to this: *the man of intellect* "must knowingly reduce himself to an unlimited refusal to be anything whatsoever." Thus in order to achieve absolute self-awareness, we must tear ourselves away from nature and life, we must constantly negate them in ourselves. Seen from this angle Valéry might be defined as a mystic of a strange kind, infinitely anxious to free himself from all emotional and spiritual life (in the usual sense), a mystic of self-awareness, "daughter of faceless being."

Many of these attitudes and directions can be waved aside or neglected as relics of the immediate past which are already rejected. On the whole, however, they may still stand as legitimate symbols, though caricatures, of the impossibility among us of an integrated attack on reality, even of our impatience with such integration. We do not yet understand that "integrity" involves a terrible asceticism which can involve more passion and strength than any romantic or violent approach to existence; nor do we realize that belief or existence cannot be conquered by violence, *or at any one salient.*

This also holds true of all forms of pure abstractionism, of inflexible assaults on any kind of pure *concept.* The unyielding passion with which Communism pursues the logic and infallibility of its own system is the case in point which Arthur Koestler has dramatized in his *Darkness at Noon.*

2. THE ISOLATED INTELLIGENCE

In the following remarks I do not take the liberal mentality as the problem, but only as one out of many manifestations of the general tendency to exalt this intelligence as the only possible source of light. We can witness on many levels this exaltation of the isolated person, accompanied as it is by an assault on frozen and corrupt forms of outer reality.

For, actually, it was the historical and not the metaphysical essence of society that originally caused the break of many intellectuals away from the idea of human society. That they should have rebelled against certain historical forms, with their deep layers of injustice and decay, was understandable; that the reaction should in subtle ways have become metaphysical (against the very idea of society) was tragic.

The story of the liberal is to be told not only in terms of the past and the forms he has rejected, but also in terms of the present and the immediate future, that is to say, in terms of the forms of society he is now asked to choose between.

All his fears, his suspicions, his spiritual problems are told in the penetrating novel, *Middle of the Journey*, by Lionel Trilling. Perhaps such a book will not be understood at all a hundred years hence, but meantime it can be taken as a fairly classical expression of much of the epistemological tragedy of modern man. The hero, John Laskell, cannot act in the direction of insertion because he is not convinced. On the other hand, he cannot be convinced without some form of insertion into at least some of the lesser analogical forms of society. His whole being relaxes only when in the presence of some form of the "naive," where he gets the taste of action and of community. Now this presence takes the form of that unique awareness of being that goes with a period of convalescence; now in the presence of a nurse whose whole character is full of simple, straightforward intellection and decision; again in the presence of a man who, in a mystical language of grunts to animals, acts as though there were no barriers between the different levels of nature; finally in the presence of a real man of this world, one who takes craftsmanship and sin and evil and drink in stride and in whom there are no questions. These are all analogies and symbols of that mutual "belonging" and organicism that should mark the relations between cosmos, society and person. But they are stray, evanescent, ineffective, and it would take a thousand more of them, something that at least vaguely resembles a "culture," before the complicated being of a John Laskell, with all its subterranean loneliness, might find real belonging and relaxation. Indeed, all that we are saying is that the problem of the creation of a culture and the epistemological problem are often related. But meantime the nature and necessity of culture and community were obscured for many of the intellectuals by what they conceive to be forces of the will, swings of the pendulum from Marxian innocence to mystical communities of guilt. Above all, they are afraid of the idea of *power* and are scandalized by it. They have an equal distrust of the "leaps" of Kierkegaard and all the existentialists, the savage "will" of Marxism, and the "power" of the Church.

Thus they hold on with "ferocity" and "tenacity" (these are the two words of Laskell) to their own position, and the difficulty is that they will themselves, exalting such a lonely position, constitute a vacuum into which, given the occasion and their own basic weakness, the most terrible forces can rush.

II

Are we correct in saying that the existence of a healthy society and a culture is an invaluable help for the normal solution of the problem of belief? If so, then we can very well transfer at least part of the responsibility for unbelief to the Christian wherever he fails to "enter the city" to construct such a society and culture. This subject requires considerable discussion, and I should like in this second half of our analysis to advance the following notes as a partial analysis of the problem. Throughout them we shall be first concerned with natural belief, but in such a way as not to exclude the supernatural.

THE EXISTENTIAL PROTEST

Existentialism, in the sense of a narrow modern philosophical school, seems on the downgrade at the moment and I for one think that it is just as well. What I should like to do here is to indicate that one of its values was to have stressed an all-important vein of the epistemological problem and that, thereafter, having reopened the vein, it became false to its own vocation by closing every possible answer to the question.

A good deal of the existential philosophy consisted of a vigorous protest against the excessively conceptual and mathematical statement of the epistemological question. It had framed a strong criticism of the idea of man as a purely epistemological animal, as a creature who can *know,* whose mind can function, no matter what the status of the remainder of his personality and no matter what his relation to the existential world by which he is surounded or to that existence out of which he himself is inwardly compounded.

If, for example, man is a purely epistemological animal, if it is some kind of "pure mind" that knows, how do we struggle out of a world of pure concepts and come in contact with "the existent"? Kierkegaard had tried to highlight the problem in a dramatic way by denying that we could know Christianity without *being* Christians. He would go so far as to identify knowledge with existence. This is only an exaggerated statement of an old Augustinian truth. But others became more carefully interested in a more technical and more hardheaded analysis of the more traditional question, How does the epistemological animal come in contact with existence? Here there is a common bond in the answer as it began to be outlined by such men as Gabriel Marcel, Berdyaev and Jaspers. With these three there is a common meeting of minds in denying the very possibility of either a mind or a concept that is itself isolated from existence. These are themselves existents and they know reality in terms of this existence. Thus we are already in contact with a first, fundamental relation of analogy between subject and object.

All the unique phrases and themes of these thinkers revolve around the central idea of the return of thought itself to existence. There is the common protest against the uprooting of the mind from the rest of the personality, from the body, from the world. There is the attack on the depersonalizing of thought and the consequent exaltation of the "mathematical" system. There is the insistence that the mind itself is not a pure spectator but is involved in, and committed to, existence. Nor is this existence itself an abstraction; rather, it is a highly specific and concrete situation, sometimes appalling in its specificity and *irrationality*. This has led to the charge from many philosophers that existentialism is not a metaphysics and that it can never come in contact with *existence itself*.

I should say that the general force of much of the existential critique had been to say that, once we transfer existence outside of thought, the problem of contact with, and penetration into, existence becomes insoluble. We should have identified knowledge exclusively with the concept and with Euclidean answers to "problems."

Philosophers were quick to answer that the traditional philosophy had already solved the problem by placing the subject in the order of existence. Knowledge of existence is possible indeed because our cognitive operations, as Gilson puts it, presuppose the vital experience of existents *by an existent*. Knowledge "is the act of an operation which corresponds to an act of existence." It is "an act which corresponds to an act." Thus, in relation to this question, there is no difficulty. They would, on the other hand, lodge two general charges against the new philosophy. The latter is satisfied with a pure sensation of existence, deprived of concepts or intelligibility. It is no wonder, therefore, that existentialism can define existence in terms of naked experience, anguish, *nausée*, the absurd. Again, the charge would continue, they have completely existentialized knowledge. It is the integrity of his own being, his sincerity or authenticity, his subjectivity, the modality of his knowing, which matters entirely for man the knower. It is not the "that which" but the "how" of knowledge which matters.

I should like, with others, to add to this summarizing criticism by suggesting that, yes, the first crime of many of the existentialists had been to close the door on essence, which is the only light we have into existence. But this disease took a peculiarly savage shape in failing to relate itself to the essences and actualities of society and history. There is no one who feels more than the Christian that he is a part of these two realities and they a part of him. And there is no more effective way of rendering difficult the ingress to belief for the kind of people we are talking about than by eradicating these two essences. The metaphysics of St. Thomas was a metaphysics of analogy. And I am suggesting for discussion that these intellectuals, among other reasons because their gift of intelligence has been given by God for society, need the analogies of society and history precisely as helps to understand this higher analogy.

With this much as background, let me propose the three categories that seem to me actually to enter into the final formation of many human certainties. They will be discussed under the terms *organicism, analogy* and *personality*.

ORGANICISM

The larger the field of activity the personality has, the greater will be its insights into reality. The person is inserted into a given actuality of being. His total socio-historical situation is precisely the concrete terms of the word "existence" as it is used above to describe the actuality of the thinking mind. His insertion into reality, as it extends itself, will indeed be accompanied by an increasing sense of the depth of self; and it is with the growth of these two polarities, of exteriority and interiority, that a real sense of certainty is grasped and grows with relation to such ultimate metaphysical concepts as being, the Absolute and Love as principles of the universe. It is only to the degree that we insert ourselves into the world and accept it that it is possible for us to become truly intellectual. Otherwise there are dichotomies in our persons that make thinking and certitude about first principles difficult. For we shall be rejecting being on one plane (the socio-historical) and trying to find it and understand it on another (the transcendent).

What is needed for insight into transcendent existence by the apparently isolated intelligence is the growing and broadening affirmation of existence in its concrete forms by the total personality. And this, once again, is one definition that might be given to the term "existent subject" in the epistemological problem. Thus, in this attempt to explain the full value of the epistemological position of St. Thomas, we are also confronting the metaphysics of St. Augustine, that, namely, "we must be in the truth before we know it."

ANALOGY

Actually, however, this affirmed existence will be seen to take the forms of structures or categories resident in *our* existence, which correspond analogically to the final insights, first principles, and systems of metaphysics and theology that have traditionally stood as the apex of human thought and search. It is perfectly true that existence, as *we* have it, is a pure *donnée,* one out of many possibilities, and is, in that sense, what we technically call an "irrational." But even here the principle of analogy will hold, for this reality of the "irrational" is itself a constant reflexion of the principle of *freedom* and personality and choice that operates in and behind the universe. But there are also various structures and intelligible forms resident in this irrational, which are recognizable in many different fields and on many different heirarchical levels of the actual. Such final metaphysical principles as the contingent-absolute relationship, freedom, love, can best be understood and accepted in terms of corresponding analogies in the structure of our own being—in the large sense in which we have defined the latter. It is only necessary to give one or two examples here, for it is the task of specialists to explore the real for analogies with the instrument of the concrete, critical, penetrating intelligence. I am thinking, for example, of a possible view of the basic spirituality of history, its easy comprehension in the Platonic terms of the evanescent and thoroughly contingent individual who participates in the eternal and recurring and enduring and emerging reality of constant organic wholes, so that individuals never occur save in terms of wholes or organisms or forms. I believe that, *mutatis mutandis,* the same thing is true of the movement of the electron. Actually, we cannot talk here of transitional movement; we can discover only different absolute positions. The contingent, therefore, is never discoverable anywhere save in terms of the most rigorous "absolutes." But my feeling in general is that there are a thousand and one both obvious and subtle forms of the analogy of the contingent-absolute formula to be found in nature and in ourselves.[2] Nor would I wish in any sense to confine my remarks to the limited area of science in the question of analogy. For there has been a development of the analogical

[2] About the created or finite analogies we have been speaking of, two things may be said: a) they can generate a mentality capable of understanding the analogy of being of the metaphysics of Aquinas, which is a study of the relation of the finite-infinite; b) they are an analogy of this analogy and must be fitted into the structure of the latter. Thus, as we shall see later, it was the major intention of Plato as an educator to forge a soul capable of understanding, and sympathetic to, the One of metaphysics and theology. And this may clarify for the reader the frequently analogous use of the idea of analogy in this chapter!

instinct in many directions, even as a method of exploring the depths of the nature of man.

We might very well also take into account the meaning of a man like Baudelaire in poetry, with his sense of the connaturality, the analogical kinship, the mutual self-revelation, that exist between things and man. Claudel, again, is the great poetic teacher of analogy and of the symbolism of creation on the very widest scale.

Of course, a doctrine and habit of analogy, like everything else, has its dangers. One difficulty comes from the fact that there are so many varied personal and racial forms of sensibility which capture so many different analogies. The whole temperament, life-history and set of talents of each individual determine *his* way of seeing things. One man may have no dialectical gift at all, but his whole personality and mind may come alive in the shape of images, concrete forms, symbols. So, too, with different total cultures. They are different social incarnations of the power of the mind to form a view, a manner, a spirit of seeing. In general we may equate analogy with the gift of *sensibility,* or awareness; and modern man is surely characterized by a growing sensibility and a capacity to understand or create many analogical expressions of reality, whether cultural of mathematical or artistic.

But we must note that in addition to the temptation resident in every gift of genius to break through existence with this gift, there is also the opposing danger, proceeding from this multiformed ability to sympathize with many avenues into the real, of concluding that "There is no one Truth 'with unalterable and fixed foundations in nature.' " The modern intelligence is inclined to sit back and adore its own suppleness, its own analogical multiplicity, or that suppleness of reality by which the latter forms an infinite number of systems and organisms. It is liable to confuse the idea of sympathy with integration.

If, therefore, the capacity for analogy is a blessing, it is not too much to say that it can become, and has often been, a curse and a disease. The gift of sensibility is here to stay, but it desperately needs the most careful kind of dialectic and metaphysics: for any civilization that gives up the gift of dialectic will not fare well. The Christian metaphysician can accompany the march of the concrete, penetrating intelligence by building up a correct metaphysics of analogy and a psychology of sensibility that will safeguard the nature of truth.

One very important point to be stressed here, however, is that we must not allow our idea of analogy, as here used, to degenerate ironically into its very opposite. Mr. Francis Fergusson, in his excellent book to which I have referred in other connections, *The Idea of a Theater,* suggests that basically there are two different types of dramatic art, the one "analogical," the other "univocal." The former creates a unified action, all the elements of which participate in the structure of the organism but preserve their own identities and related lines of action. The other (the univocal) reduces all its component elements to *illustrations* of an idea, a mood, an action. The univocal system would imply that there is an overhead reality which can stand on its own two feet, but which can very well use limitless ornamentation and illustrative material. Actually, therefore, for it the analogies are not part of the artistic system or idea, but are exterior to it.[3]

---

[3] In all fairness, therefore, this kind of habit pervades more fields of thought than the metaphysical. Some literary critics are chary, for example, of any formulas or principles of criticism and would insist that each literary fact is *toto caelo* different from any other. For them, all critical systems are so many nominalistic and empty forms. This would, indeed, be the case, if all such "formulas" were not in fact expressions which have no meaning apart from the total series of cases to which they refer and through which they run in a partly-the-same, partly-different manner. Thus the use of the idea "all poetry is

Thus all such material is reduced to the level of the unimportant, has no identity save as illustration; you might say it is a mere function after the manner of a proletariat in an economic system that revolves independently of human persons. Mr. Fergusson's book has been appraised as one of the most important contributions to modern literary criticism and the author has acknowledged that it is strongly indebted to the analogical realism of St. Thomas. It is but one example of the endless ways in which that doctrine can and should fructify. This analogy of being is in a way a sketch of the mentality and the reality of the Western tradition at its best: a world where everything is seen as chock-full of its own reality and importance but also able to participate in larger communities of reference; where all things have meaning and transcendent reference *and* actuality in their own right. Perhaps the two things most opposed to it are the completed, self-contained fact of modern science on the one hand (where meaning and transcendence are bad manners) and the myth of the system in communism on the other (where the actuality of the individual is lost). The habit of analogy can have a dozen signs: the survival of the person even though (and because) he participates in society; the actuality of the metaphor in poetry; the reality of the single actor or event in total play or novel; even the appeal of Charles Malik of Lebanon that the West not only actuate itself more liberally

---

dramatic" by T. S. Eliot has no meaning or use if it is univocal, for it both changes and develops its meaning on every level of poetry and with every poem. Actually, the work of the concrete critic should always illuminate and develop the meaning of the philosophical critic, and the two types of work should form but one body of meaning. The ideal would be that they should be incorporated in the work of one person, should, indeed, proceed from the single act of a single mind. We should never under any circumstances accept the opposition of a sect of abstract principles and a corresponding set of concrete insights.

on the politico-economic plane but also that it find its old, traditional points of transcendence over this level before it is too late.

Indeed, could we not even go so far as to say that the habit of analogy is implicitly Christian. I should suggest that, with its emphasis on actuality and meaning, it is the natural school of Christians. It is at the heart of metaphysics and, in a not too poetic sense, of Christianity. For it tends to create the two basic attitudes of the Christian, that of the martyr in the name of the historic actuality of the Christian mysteries, and that of the lover of meanings, who does not hesitate to relate these actualities to the whole universe.

The truth is, then, that first of all, as St. Thomas says, and as commentators such as Gilson insist, the thinking subject is in the order of existence and so is his thought. It is through his own location in this order that he touches the existing object and "recognizes" it. In fact, there is a constant interchange between subject and object. The object is known and recognized in terms of the existence of the subject, and the subject knows itself, and comes more intimately to know itself, through the object. But this interchange can only hold if there is a constant connaturality and analogical kinship between man and the world. In fact, it is this basic analogy between subject and object that makes any act of knowledge possible and valid.

PERSONALITY

One way of conceiving the development of an analogical system is that the analogies discovered in created reality do not remain as so many objects to be known and contemplated by an intelligence that is otherwise external to them. It is better to think that, as a result of man's acceptance of them and his insertion into the orders of actuality and morality which are involved in them, they become part of his own existence, of his own personality; they are the incarnated enlargement of his own being. This holds true not only for his insights and his "acts," but also for his creations. A literary work is, for example, only a verbalization of his own being, an analogue of himself, and immediately there is set up another analogical kinship between subject and work of art, each illuminating the being of the other and serving all the purposes of the person-state relationship created by Plato in the *Republic*. This kind of aesthetics of the person is directly at odds with that "heresy of aesthetics" which would make of the work of art a separate *object* to be judged on its own terms and which makes so philosophically difficult the kind of moral criticism that now begins to emerge among literary men.

Thus concrete perception, moral action, artistic creation and insertion into society become all one total personal system within which we live and by the help of which the actualities of belief can be grasped even more vitally; only let us remember that it is the *mind* that is doing the grasping, whether it be by the formal comprehension of the truth or by our own connaturality with it.

Of all these sources of analogy, the human community is the most important; in a sense it is the sum of all of them. Epistemologically, man is like a child outside of society. Outside of it his mind cannot grow. The analogies of personality and freedom, of home and redemption, of the laying down of life for one's friends, are the sources of final understanding and are hardly to be found elsewhere. This is especially true for the intellectual, for there is between the man of intelligence and society a mutual give and take that nourishes the mind and the being of each. But one of the great tragedies of our time is the separation of the two, of the man of intelligence from the people. The whole vocation of the former is to give light to the people; but he will himself seldom find light in any other source. And thus, whenever we turn in this discussion, we come back again to the moving words of Dostoevski that have already been cited above.

It will be clear that, throughout this section, I have been using a number of ideas which are Platonic; the two most important of these are "analogy" and recognition (or recollection). In general the species of analogy in the epistemology of Plato has been given scant attention, even though, for example, it forms the very substance of his thought in the *Republic*. If one of the functions of that work is to explore the hypothesis of a principle of unity and goodness in and behind the universe, the whole drive of its educational system is to create those analogies in the order of knowledge and personality which will make recognition of these Ideas possible. The elements entering into this picture are limitless. They include an endless number of critical perceptions of form in the arts and the whole culture life of the Greek city state, an exploration of all the analogical unities in mathematics, astronomy and the other sciences, a subjection to a thorough moral and ascetical training, an insertion into the great analogue of human society—all this before the subject is capable of any kind of philosophical insight that will be something more than a children's game. It is in terms of this total pre-experience that the Platonic theory of recollection and memory must be understood, not in terms of some superficial and purely symbolic myth of pre-existence. It is unnecessary to repeat again how the Thomistic ideas of analogy and connaturality perform a similar service in these pages.

Only one other thing should be said here. It may be difficult for the nonbeliever to achieve belief without courage. And there is nothing so brave as intellectual courage. It is much easier to believe with the will and the affections, to leap with Kierkegaard, to believe with the stomach, with tricks, with jumps into the hands of God—easier to believe thus than with the mind. It is easy to talk about commitment, but if we do not commit the mind we commit little. And that is one of the fascinating things about Catholicism, its periodic insistence on the power of the human mind to know.

One advantage of this kind of theorizing on the act of knowledge, above all on the act of knowledge called connaturality, is that, rather than weakening, it supports and completely justifies the act of belief of the ordinary man. The insertion of the simple soul into society and life, its affirmations of existence, its consequent grasp interiorly of a subtle multiplicity of analogies, often far outweigh the purely conceptual and mathematical skill of the more gifted, who approach the ultimate affirmation of existence with divided personalities, uprooted from the community. It is the integrated personality (not integration in terms of the "foursquare" man of the Renaissance idea, but *integration into the real*) who can best "know." This is one of the senses in which knowledge is communicated to society and not to the isolated intellectual. It is given to the social person.

Nevertheless, a final word on *responsibility*. There is not merely the question here of discovering analogies. There is the necessity of creating them. If we do not have a concrete Christian culture replete with such analogies, that is partially because of the retreat of the Christian from existence.

One might be tempted, therefore, to say that the philosophical and theological theorist must play a humble role in the problem of belief. At least in our time. For the main task, the neglected task, is the creation by field workers, by men of resolute action and creative imagination, of the infinite bits of analogy that go to the formation of a culture and a society.

But this would be a superficial and unfortunate view, and only true as far as it goes. Only souls that are profoundly Christian, that are lost and saturated in the mystery of Christianity, will be able to act creatively and purely, without stain, without impurity, in the existential order of society. Indeed, Archbishop Feltin, successor to Cardinal Suhard, in his address to the Convocation of Catholic Intellectuals of France, solemnly placed the first responsibility for the solution of the tortuous relations between nature and grace, humanism and the supernatural, society and God, on the shoulders of the theologians. In America there is a healthy drive which recognizes the need of the Christian purification and reformation of our human society. But what must be just as strong and is as intensely necessary is a profoundly eschatological movement in life and theology. These reforms are impossible unless Christianity, ascetically and theoretically, is first caught with clarity in all its purity. This would seem to be the very reverse of the thesis of the present chapter, but I do not think that is so. In fact, what would now be very desirable would be a discussion of the great importance of a powerful theological force in American Catholicism, and of the relation of such a force to the rebirth of a Christian society. We have said that there is, or should be, a vitalizing give and take between society and the intellectual. But among Christians the same give and take should also hold true between the theologians and the Christian social thinker. Indeed, there could be no more beautiful collaboration than this, so far as the intellectual who is alienated from society and from God is concerned. For we should then be remembering that he is not necessarily a critic or an enemy, but a man whose mind and whole personality needs a home.

6

Toward a Theatre of Public Action

It may seem farfetched to discuss the absence of ritual drama in our modern theatre within a book that has attempted to deal with "larger" problems.

There is a sense, however, in which no problem is larger than the false dichotomy presently posed between the private and public in art, or the equally false dichotomy between art and life—however variously these terms may be defined. It is for this reason that I feel impelled to have the concluding chapters of this book deal with one general and one specific aspect of the totalistic temptation in the area of artistic creation and reception. In that context, I trust, a discussion of the collapse of ritual drama will appear quite relevant to any discussion of the metaphysical illnesses of modern man.

I

One difference between our theatrical situation and the old ritual situations is the presence or absence of a *style,* a set of accepted rhythms and choreographical movements that is deeper than, but the basis of, our set conception of rhythm and dance. Now, in our day, where style is present, we have to create it anew each time that we do attempt to fix it into our theatre. Martha Graham makes it on her own. George Balanchine makes it on his own (though he at least can fall back on a basic vocabulary of movement). In the brilliant *West Side Story* Jerome Robbins makes it on his own and it may not happen again so well for another half generation. It is not in the air. We publicly despise public style. If DeGaulle has it, many of us fall back on the defense that this form of greatness is the greatness of a clown. The theatre is often a private place for the private investigation of the private soul. We wish to build a great national cultural center in Washington and we blame Congress for not getting behind the idea. Rightly. But the inhibition of the Congress is our own inhibition. As a nation and a people, we are against these rhythms, this style and this context of impersonal greatness. No, it is better to say that we are afraid of it and have ganged up in a new ritual against it. A ritual against ritual. It is at least possible that the explanation is that we are afraid of closeness, afraid because the level of it we have, the conformities we have to live with, are indeed destructive of personality. As a result we have little in our lives that implies a public action, a rite of any kind, a moving and acting together. And lest it be understood that we are only talking of religious rites, let me say that I am also very much thinking of the purely social and political orders.

But it is at least very heartening to note that this question of the necessity and possibility of common movement as a nation and a community is now the subject of intense discussion and debate. We *are* asking the critical questions. How much of our economy is being devoted to public over against private purposes? Are we losing and can we regain our national sense of purpose as a community? Is the Presidency just another among many functions which must carefully mind its own business or is it the center of moral leadership for the nation? Can we any longer exist alone internationally? Is there any way to recover our own greatness and confidence as a people than to turn outward internationally toward the underdeveloped countries? Can any person or institution or nation stay healthy without turning outward toward an increasingly public act?

These questions seem to be social and political questions and not literary or theatrical questions. But I think they are the latter too. For we are thinking and talking of that public style of life and thought without an insertion into which a theatre must always remain very limited and "personal," in the pejorative sense of that word, and without which it can never produce or recreate the rituals of public action. The personal purifications that we are in the habit of associating with the actions of great theatre (those of Oedipus, Prometheus, Hamlet, Lear) are never truly such unless they move in some way or other back into the public order. But the opposite kind of literary action and purification, of which we are often in danger, is that of Ulysses as he is portrayed in *The Odyssey: A Modern Sequel* of Kanzantzakis. There the movement is toward a completely solipsistic moment, toward a purification which purifies the actor of any association with reality and the public order.

II

Even on the level of pure language, the relation between the theatre and the literary on the one hand and the public order, the social, the political, on the other, is there. I certainly do not wish to question the fact that poets and men of the theatre are creative. We can also agree with Eliot that they are also always purifying the language of the tribe. We can agree with the existentialists that the people are always in danger, as indeed we all are, of becoming a great impersonal *one,* a they, a mass, a set of chatterers of inconsequential things, destroying ideas and rhythms or not interested in them. The poets and persons must fight against this. But surely, true though all this may be, it is only a half and not the better half of the truth. For the people also create a language; it *is* a public as well as a personal action. We can recall here the controversy between Rosemond Tuve and William Empson as an example. Mr. Empson lauded the private invention and genius of George Herbert, as well he might. But for Miss Tuve, Empson had made the serious mistake of failing to realize or talk about the wonderful creativity for language and multi-meaning of that whole popular community which Herbert was falling back upon. We all make language. In fact some children have to be slapped down for making it too much.

We must always be aware of the moment when either of the two elements in this interpenetrating creative task, the public order or the creative individual, is going awry or is not doing its job, but we get nowhere by insisting that the one or the other must do the whole job. And right now all I am saying is that our own theatre often inclines, by very necessity, to go without the help of the public order, to fall back almost completely on privacy and on what we might call the highly personal. Actually this is a very general tendency even outside of the theatre, even within what we would hope would be a style and public order. We seem to be increasingly obsessed with the private.

III

We have made a general decision, both press and the people, that we have an absolute right to the stimulation of the private, and of course the private means the privacy of other people. I am not saying that the most private and the most interior nature of man does not by right belong to the work of the artist; nevertheless it seems pretty clear that art is beginning to fall back on this notion of the psychiatric private in a rather special and specious way. There are a number of plays I can think of, and so can you, which are indeed very powerful, but there is good reason to conclude that the kind of power they are falling back upon is that of the psychiatric case book. Such "cases" have a very obvious intensity and allure in the way of sharpness and stimulation, and they need very little redoing or shaping by the intelligence or sensibility of the artist in order to reach the goal of intensity.

I cannot help but think that this is true of a good deal of the art of Eugene O'Neill. And I wonder if it is not true of at least some of the work of Arthur Miller. Here let me quote some summarizing sentences from an article in *The Sewanee Review* by Henry Popkin.

. . . Miller's plays have moved steadily inward. Although each play has probed the impact of large, bewildering issues upon a simple man, the large issues have become increasingly dim. Some of the haziness is intrinsic, but some of it is induced by the simple man's mounting personal problems. In *All My Sons,* the issue is no less than the war itself. The play shares the weakness of its chief character, who finds it hard to make the war's values immediate and meaningful. *Death of a Salesman* strikes a balance between the social problem of the shattered myth of success and Willy Loman's sex and family problems. *The Crucible* shows us witch hunts, but the obvious contem-

porary reference is masked by the historical setting and by
the very distinctive seventeenth-century speech; what remains is
the tension between the incalculable malice of private individuals and the conscience of a guilt-ridden husband. With *A
View from the Bridge,* Miller's focus moves still further within.
Eddie Carbone is not only troubled and guilty; he is sick, and
his symptoms resemble those that Tennessee Williams, the most
typically "internal" of contemporary American dramatists, had
made the common substance of Broadway drama—incestuous
inclinations, psychotic sexual jealousy, frenzied hostility to
homosexuality, and possibly incipient homosexuality. If these
symptoms are present, it is less important that the immigration
service also has its shortcomings; the play's main topic has become Eddie's troubles.

These materials are only examples and I think there are
few who will question the fact that the examples could be
multiplied endlessly. I have suggested in an analysis of our
popular culture that we may very well find that the same
problems of the imagination exist on the two levels of popular and intellectual culture, though they exist on two different levels of refinement. One of these problems is the
notion of arts as immediate excitement, and I am not sure that
the intellectual is not as guilty in his refined way of this
affliction as the mass media are in their way. Here we see
him at it in the form of his dedication to the attractions of
the absolutely inward and private. But surely it is sensible
to maintain that even here he defeats his own purposes. For
it is not possible ever to penetrate the private and the personal if we limit responses to the latter and do not see, as
Dante did, the great analogies of the personal interior life
on the levels of history, the social, the political, and the
theological. We seem almost on the verge theatrically of concluding that a public action, an action of the community,

must be necessarily superficial, and that it is only by a penetration, usually violent, of the purely interior that we can really master the secrets of the human reality.

I have always felt that it is with some such suppositions as these that we instinctively approach the idea of ritual theatre. But surely art itself is far more than the personal in this pejorative and limited sense of the word that we have been using. In this connection I have come across a very happy summary of the problem as Arthur Mizener reintroduces us to one of the great novels of our time, *The Fathers* of Allen Tate:

The central tension of *The Fathers,* like that of its structure, is a tension between the public and the private life, between the order of civilization, always artificial, imposed by discipline, and at the mercy of its own imperfections, and the disorder of the private life, always sincere, imposed upon by circumstances, and at the mercy of its own impulses. We see, on the one hand, the static condition a society reaches when, by slow degrees, it has disciplined all personal feeling to custom so that the individual no longer exists apart from the ritual of society and the ritual of society expresses all the feelings the individual knows. We see, on the other hand, the forces that exist—because time does not stand still—both within and without the people who constitute a society, that will destroy the discipline of its civilization and leave the individual naked and alone.

IV

Let us go one step further in this analysis of and exploration into the nature and possibility of some kind of ritual theatre for the future. Let us take a further look at the idea of the purely personal over against the concept of art as in some way or other a public act. And let us here fall back

upon Nietzsche for an understanding of part of the problem
we are up against. For Nietzsche Greek tragedy, and can we
not say with him the very nature of art, involves a unity and
a reconciliation between Dionysus and Apollo. At any rate
Dionysus can represent for us all the powerful but yet un-
formed elements in the soul and life of man that have not
yet been touched by Apollo, that is by the mastering and
forming genius of the artist. In other words Dionysus has
not yet become a formal and public act, and here for the
first time I use the phrase *a public action* in all its possible
metaphorical senses as well as its literal sense. The first passion of the artist, as Dionysus gives it to us, has not yet
achieved that further moment of passion which rhythm and
number can give to it. Similarly with movement. The first
movements of Dionysus, that is to say the first acts of sensibility of the artist, are passionate and brilliant. But who is
there to say that the choreography of the Greeks and the
choreography of the Church took away from that passion and
did not add to it?

Let us just keep adding all the elements that go into the
construction of the public act of the great artists. So far we
have taken a rapid glance at rhythm and choreography as
they added themselves to the personal without making the
personal less personal.

Now let us look at the other possible levels of a possible
ritual play for the future. Let us for example remind ourselves of how Plato mastered the understanding and creation
of the person in the *Republic*. He added the level of the
social and the political, after having persuaded himself that
the human community is only the soul itself written out in
large letters, the soul made public but not in the sense of
the invasion of privacy. Let us listen to Plato as he thinks
out the relationship between the shape of the individual soul
and the shape of the human community. And as we listen

let us remember that we would not be doing him justice if we do not remember at the same time that he had the same concern as do we, the interior and precious image of human personality. But he knows that introspection, though it is a good way, is also a dark and limited way and must be buttressed by other forms of search. It is in this spirit that in the Second Book of the *Republic* Socrates speaks:

". . . The search we undertake is no small matter, but one that needs a sharp eye, as it seems to me. Well then, since we are not clever, I think," said I, "that we should make the following kind of search for our object. Suppose we had been told by someone to read an inscription in small letters a good way off, and we had not very sharp sight; and then someone noticed the same inscription somewhere else, in larger letters on a larger tablet, that would be a great piece of luck, I think. We could read the large ones first, and then examine the smaller, to see if they were the same."

"That's true enough," said Adeimantos, "but what do you see like it in the search about justice?"

"I'll tell you," said I. "There is justice of one man, we say, and justice of a whole city, I suppose?"

"Certainly."

"Well, a city is larger than one man?"

"Of course it is," he said.

"Then perhaps there would be a larger justice in the city and easier to understand. If you like, then, let us enquire first what it is in the cities; then we will examine it in the single man, looking for the likeness of the larger in the shape of the smaller."

"That is a good proposal," said he.

"Then," said I, "suppose we should imagine we see a city in the making, we might see its justice, too, in the making, and the injustice?"

"Possibly," he said.

"So when it is made, there is hope to see what we seek more easily?"

"Yes, a good hope."

"Then ought we to try to do this task? I think it will be no small labour."

As Plato is clearly conceiving the matter in the above citation, this is a profound concept of the State and the political and the human community which we seem to have lost. We are tempted in our day to conceive of the State as an enemy; we are inclined to view the human community as a threat to personality rather than as the larger and public body for the interior of man. Thus the Greeks ultimately saw no difference between the two great sciences of Ethics and Politics. But we do and the question is, Has our way of seeing the matter profoundly affected the theatre?

Is it possible that it is some such wide-ranging difficulties and questions as these that are making difficult the rebirth, in our day and according to our own ways, of some form of a ritual theatre, a theatre of public action?

7

THEOLOGY AND HUMAN SENSIBILITY

Once we get past the difficulty of vocabulary and camp differences, we are all very much bothered by the state of art and by the state of the mass media in our civilization. For that reason, I think it would be a mistake to try to define words too accurately at the very beginning of our subject; nevertheless, let me make a few roughly summarizing statements about the two word *theology* and *sensibility*.

Let us agree that theology is the study of and the concern for the relations between man and God. As for the word *sensibility*, all I mean for the moment is that whole wide-ranging world of human feeling and reaction to the reality of things and persons and God which has always been a special preoccupation of the artist and which he has always laboured to create, refine, preserve and make grow in a refined and straight way. Perhaps *sensibility* is not the best word to represent what we shall be talking about, but it is impossible to find the perfect word in this case. If I fall back on such words as *taste* or *culture,* there will be even more trouble from groups that apparently do not approve of either. But what we are talking about is not a cute, esoteric phenomenon;

rather it is so completely central a human affair that the very men who would object most to our present vocabulary would, like all of us, explode in wrath if it were suggested to them that they had no feelings.

A man may deride the idea of taste, but his reaction will be very distasteful if you tell him that he has no taste. He is against the intellectuals until you insult him by telling him he isn't one. And he will only be against the idea of culture as long as he does not understand that that is what his father and mother had before the new culture engineers of the mass media came along to take it away from him.

All this may be a very good thing for us to remember when we discuss the positive and creative problems of our movie civilization in the United States. In concerning ourselves with the creative aspects of the movies, we do not intend to minimize the importance of what we might call the question of immediate morality, or of censorship, or of all those brief two-minute movie sequences that are objectionable to fundamental morality. These are problems and they are being dealt with. But we must also have a concern for more widespread and ultimately more serious questions that deal with the creative or non-creative state of the other ninety-eight minutes of each cinema production.

I think that the science called tactics is very important and it is therefore the purpose of these remarks to urge that there is another position which we should *not* adopt. That would be the position of improvers, reformers or crusaders; I mean specifically improvers of or crusaders among the people. I have no fear of a crusade against the culture engineers of our mass media who have taken so powerful a grip on the national imagination. But I would gently warn both myself and others that our relation to the people must be quite different. If we come to them as improvers and reformers, we will be coming to them as from the outside and as superior, and they will have none of us. They need and will accept teachers, but teachers whom they have themselves begotten and with whom they have deep bonds of understanding and affection. Let us not be beaten so easily in this science of who is on whose side. Christianity has always been on the side of the people, and vice versa. But by their present successful tactic the engineers and exploiters have persuaded a good fraction of the people that they are on the popular side; that they are the only ones who speak the people's language, that they know what people like, that they, poor things, are being treated roughly by the critics and the intellectuals and are therefore in a state of common grievance with the people. I believe that these engineers are indeed exploiting the people in the name of the cheap, but I am adding to this the reflection that there is such a thing as exploiting the people in the name of the good. There is such a thing as an attitude that culturally the people are fundamentally hopeless, but we will deceive them away from their real convictions in the name of the good—we will bait them away from what they really like, we who alone know the answers. Fortunately it is not necessary to get into such a weak and artificial position, and we will certainly not get far if we do not believe fundamentally in men and women. It is a pretty sure thing that, before a more specialized view of literature and the arts arose among us, the great artists explored the hearts of people for their materials and only differed from them finally in that they were able to say for men and women what the latter were not able to say for themselves.

On the other hand, it must be admitted that if this confidence and this view about the fundamentally healthy instincts of the popular level are wrong, then they are very wrong and we risk wasting great energy in the name of a dream. We ought to face that fact and ask ourselves what we think. If I may be forgiven a few personal sentences, the one recurring criticism of my book on the subject, *The Image Industries,* was that this was a romantic view and that the book was out of touch with the reality of things and the nature of people. I must say that I did my best to correct this difficulty from my earliest childhood. I got myself deliberately born on the east side of New York and, spent the first twenty years of my life in sometimes questionable surroundings. Actually I sincerely believe that this is not at all important and that the people of the east side of New York can be just as snobbish as people born in penthouses; the geography does not matter, for sooner or later we would be entering into a competition to decide who is closer to the people, a competition which can get very vulgar. Actually the only competition that matters is extremely serious: there seems to be what amounts to almost a formal statement in the national air that the commercial forces of the nation know more about man in the mass than either Christianity or the artists.

Is it too much to say that that is the whole point and the whole question at issue? We can at least agree that it is one of the great issues. This chapter is only a beginning of an attempt to establish some of the proper grounds for discussing this central question.

To eliminate unnecessary debate let us get as close to the vocabulary of commercialism as we can without violating our own sense of the dignity of religion and art. Let us admit immediately that what we all want to do is to locate the needs of men and women and to satisfy them.

What I want first to propose, as a sort of working point of discussion, is that the very deepest need the people have is the need for closeness to, union with, things and persons and God. This principle underlies every need of man. It is not a luxury or a gimmick. It is fundamental, primitive, eternal and universal. This closeness is the very air the human personality must breathe, whether it be rich or poor, with or without talent. If understood correctly this need could have no negative answers in a Trendex rating. Everybody knows, when it is put in his language, that real solitude is hell and that unity is peace. I am not speaking of togetherness or of any cheap or vulgar principle. For even the terrible need we also have to be independent is only an expression of the need we have to be close to ourselves, to have real self-identity, not to lose the taste of our own soul which is the pearl without price.

It is the passionate vocation of theology, or religion and art, real art, to satisfy, each in its own way, this tremendous need by putting men in touch with things and people and God. Theology and art are always searching for reality and are always using different techniques to *uncover* it so that we may be in touch with it. But the commercial instinct, as such, is not concerned professionally with reality, and its major instinct, as we know it in our day, is to *cover it up*. Let us keep our minds on these two ideas, to uncover and to cover. This is the central point of conflict—between commercialism and art, as well as between commercialism and religion.

Unfortunately it is not quite the common understanding that both theology and art have the common vocation of moving us into contact with reality. An altogether opposite and romantic notion of the work of both has held sway for a long time in many quarters. The image we have had of the principle work of the imagination is that, because the reality we have been surrounded with since the industrial revolution is not very interesting, we must, perforce, invent or create a better one such as has never been seen on land or sea. It has been easy to push this logic of art to its complete conclusion in the mass media of the movies and TV, where pure fantasy, the incredible images of the horror story, and the new knight on the white horse who never loses and always wins, and the great spectacular epics of Hollywood, have given us another night-time world for lack of a decent day-time one. These things may be defined as substitutes for reality. They go all the way from Disneyland and Mike Hammer to *Maverick* and *Samson and Delilah*.

I begin to think more and more that as the wind blows in the arts and in all the regions of ordinary human life, so the wind will blow in our theological reactions. It is pretty certain that we are all of one piece, and we cannot, simply cannot say that we will have a taste and a culture that will run off in this direction and have a theological direction that will run off correctly toward God. This will take a great deal of investigating, but it is worth looking into: whether or not the demands on and the insults rendered against art will not be the same as those against theology. If art is told that it is only a dream or a spectacle or a sharp sensation, theology has often enough since the nineteenth century been pushed out of the human world and told that it was transcendent and that it should stick to its own affairs. How often have we heard such phrases in our own lifetime as: politics is politics (and is not either morality or theology); business is business (just another example of a freewheeling dynamism with its own separate and non-theological laws); war is war (and it has no laws, except its own interior and non-limited laws). The clergy were told to stay out of all these things, and this was a very clever maneuver, because it made religion and the whole of the Church identical with the clergy and there was nothing easier to find at any time than a group of clergymen whose intervention in politics or business or war or anything else had been unfortunate. You could do the same for any group of men.

What I am saying is that both art and religion got themselves pushed into the same "otherworldly" and non-human status entirely against their true vocation which we have been declaring. If anything, theology suffered more than the men of the imagination from this tactic used against both. As an example we have only to read an account of the life of the wonderful Don Sturzo in Italy to see how extraordinary and faithful a combat he had to fight to re-establish the right of Christians to exist in the political order. And even art itself turned partially against theology. For, partially separated from reality as it was, it proceeded to remove itself even farther by declaring that it, too, was an entirely separate nd autonomous dynamism which had nothing to do with theology or religion. Thus even the two natural allies, allies for that drive back into reality which is so essential for modern man, became more separated than they should.

These ideas having been pretty successfully applied to the artist and the religious thinker, it was that much easier for the business mentality to rush in and maintain, to a degree never maintained before, that its type of realism and practicality should have a major place in the inner sanctum of human sensibility. This is the triple situation from which we must slowly recover.

The superficial picture that we are therefore given is that the world we are generally concerned with is divided into three parts. 1. There is first of all the religious mind, which is to be denominated as transcendental and otherworldly; which has nothing to do with immediate human realities; which at best has to do with localizable moral issues. 2. Then there is the area of the artist and his art, concerned in turn, we are told, with modes of escape from our humanity, with a vague thing called culture and taste open only to an elite intelligence. 3. There is finally the business and commercial mind which prides itself on a manly practicality and a devotion to the real order; it alone, the story goes, is in touch with the people and with things.

This is the general picture given and the vocabulary used;

this is the position into which we are tricked. What are the actual facts about these three areas of life?

Let me begin with an attempt at a partial analysis of the business mentality as it has developed in the last century. But in order to give myself the freedom to make this analysis and to remove a few inhibitions, let me say a few important preliminary things. First of all I do not wish to speak about personalities or names in this whole discussion. When I speak of the business mentality, that is only part of the mentality of any businessman. He is a human being. Further, there is in every one of us a commercial mentality that does not care for the truth. For what else is the purely commercial mentality, as it is developing among us, save that part of the soul which goes sidewise at the truth, which is willing to distort or use or exploit or even betray reality for the profit of it? And if there is a special group of men for whom this is especially true, then it can also exist in ourselves in many subtle ways. It is true of us if we are only interested in the truth when it seems to serve the interests of the Church; when we are interested in unionism only when it will seem to give good repute to the Church; when we are interested in souls only for the sake of baptismal statistics; when we join a wave of moral indignation throughout the country only if it seems called for by the rest of the wave. Having remembered that men are always men and having included and condemned ourselves, let us go on with freedom to inspect and really judge this mentality.

The supposition is that the businessman, not the religious man or the artist, is the man of reality and the man of the people. Actually one of the great problems of our civilization is the degree to which business is removed from reality. The ordinary businessman, and the ordinary white-collar worker with him, is frequently five steps removed from the final real thing with which he deals. His job deals only vaguely with the things themselves. If he invests, he invests in a number or a possibility or a name on the market. There are, today, few owners of things. There are investors and managers. There is a serious decline of the crafts among us, the crafts that work on things with the eyes and the ears and the hands. Very often when we do work on things, we work only on one part of them on an assembly line.

When pushed to an extreme, what does the pure commercial spirit do to us? It tends toward the construction of a civilization within which we do not have the completely necessary touch with existence itself that we have described as the very food of human life. When pushed to such an extreme it tends to be self-defeating and contradictory. It boasts of its efficiency and practicality and sense of reality. But it often tends to remove us out of reality and does the same thing finally to itself. It makes the body and the soul go and go and go in endless frustration ("What makes Sammy run?"). It sets up a dizzy pace that is exhausting. It is always deep down looking for something, the touch with reality, that it is itself making impossible of realization.

The very thing which the commercial part of our souls needs most is the world of art and the artist; yet it is precisely that world which its touch inclines to poison and kill. The bewildering pace of the commercial life has made art doubly necessary to our civilization, and therefore art and the culture of our civilization is the one area the commercial spirit should have stayed outside of. But it has not and the consequences of its invasion are pitiful. I do not say that businessmen should stay out of such a world because once again we must remember that they are men and many of them have contributed enormously and generously to the true culture of this nation. But the business part of the soul, theirs or ours, the part that simply wants to exploit even this precious area of life for profit, that wants to push a product, should stay out of it.

The kind of practicality that is trained to run and dominate things and people and that can so powerfully control nature is impractical and incompetent in this area. Let those who are good at these things stick to their own tasks. They are making the rest of us suffer by their invading ignorance. We will admire Madison Avenue when it sticks to its job; we will be angry when it does not. It should confine its image-making to making true images of its products and let it go at that.

Again, the commercial part of our civilization is inclined to think that money can do everything. There seems to be some compulsive idea in the air that unless you spend ten million dollars on a picture it will not be good. I think myself that if Hollywood had less money it would do better work more often. Spending so much money usually means that you spend it on gadgets and splendid insertions, and that once again you get away from the central human reality of the story or idea; thus another time and for another reason the system becomes self-defeating. The attempt to get back in touch with things is frustrated. There was a satirical comment on *The Big Fisherman's* great expenditure that it was a pity they did not have enough money to buy a New Testament. But my essential point would be that the most practical and efficient thing the image industries could do would be to confess openly their complete dependence on the true men of imagination in our culture and the men in the lonely garrets. God has given us men who can stop our mad flight and our mad running. It is the business of business to find them.

Let this be my growing theme, that what we need is reality and we cannot live without it. I once proposed this in another connection in a talk and a young man asked the question: "What is this here reality, Father?" A good and stumping question, and the only answer I could think of on the spur of the moment was, "Ask your father and mother." I will try to add to that answer, but still can't think of a better one.

Whatever reality is, in all its forms, when we get close to it, when we see with the artist what he has found, there is for the time being no need of going on with what T. S. Eliot has called distraction from distraction. I say "for the time being," and this is important, because we cannot deify the work of art, but at least it tells us that life is worth going on with, and this is the most important theological feeling a man can have. At the same time, the reality of the work of art makes unnecessary the going on and on and on in desperate wise as though we have not yet found anything of what we are after. As often as there is something of the human reality in a film or on TV, then it is no longer necessary all day and all night to keep turning and turning the channels, nor is it necessary that something flick and flick and flick before us endlessly to fill up that *horror vacui,* that horror of emptiness, of which Herbert Read has spoken. The artist has done for us what the successful doctor does with the psychotic: the artist has put us in touch. And what else will God do for us one day save that?

I should rightly be asked for examples of what I mean. I shall try to give some.

The artist carries us rhythmically and by force of a constructed action right into the heart of reality and not into the heart of a dream. The Romantics decided that their vocation was to move us out of a sordid commercial reality into the transcendent world of fantasy. But the greater artists have always moved us into the depths of the actual world we know and the world God made. Take, for example, the work of the writer of tragedy. He moves us rhythmically and powerfully by the force of successive and connected events, out of the world of false greatness deep down into the very heart of our

final weakness. Look at Oedipus, look at Lear, look at poor
Hamlet. The fantasies, the pretences, the false epic dreams
with which the play began vanish. The weakness and the
smallness is so vast that instead of vanishing into a contemptible thing it is a vast abyss of smallness. It is the region, theologically, where the *children* of God are born. But
again Mr. Eliot tells us that man cannot stand very much
reality and, therefore, the function of the artist is to imitate
the ways of God Himself in this matter, to lead us by rhythmic endurable stages to the truth, to give us only what at each
moment is good for us, and to lead us finally into a world
where there is plenty of room for God. There is contact with
ourselves at our deepest, and the result is peace, and somehow or other there is for the time being no need to flick
and flick and flick, no need to run and run and run. What
makes Sammy run? One reasonable possibility is that he
must continue to repress and not look at what the artist will
not let him repress. But what he would find is something that
in the end will not bite or destroy him. It is nothing less
than the pearl without price, his own soul. I think that this
is what the traveling circus man found at the end of the
beach in those last moments of *La Strada.* It is what the
British colonel found at the end of the rhythms of *The Bridge
on the River Kwai.* And what else did the brooding Henry
V find in that great picture; as he paced in the night before
battle in the camp of his men, what else did he find save the
souls of his fellow soldiers? It was there he found the level of
a marvelous communion between himself and his subjects,
below all the fine trappings of kings. And what else were those
five figures staring at in the final moments of *The Seventh
Seal* save the issue of death and the enormous size of the
issues for which their souls were created? He who has not
looked at death is not ready to die.

All I am trying to do in these pages is to present a theory

of the work of art as the work of uncovering reality and not of covering it. The question is worth examining and it is going to be one of our very basic quarrels with the mass media image-makers. For on the evidence of the moment they believe that reality should be covered up. True art helps us to move out of the dream into reality, and it helps us to endure the movement. The present moment of TV art and a good deal of our cinema culture is moving us out of the world into the dream. It is certainly true that the development of this kind of false and evasive sensibility in the world of culture can produce most unhappy consequences, for one thing, in the political, the military and the social orders; for the way we think in one world will be the way we think in another. We will also cover up the political, military and social realities we have to face. And that is precisely the consequence that *is* developing. And that is why the American Churches have to speak out on the enormous issues that really face American civilization. But my respectful and experimental question is, Will not people listen better to bishops if they have first listened to artists uncovering thousands and thousands and thousands of times for us the same reality as the bishops, so that at least we have the habit and the ears for listening? He who is without ears will not hear. That is the simplest definition of sensibility I can think of. *Having ears.*

If it is relatively easy to see the deep relationship between the state of our national imagination (accordingly as it drives toward a permanent state of fantasy or reality) and the level of our political, social and military wisdom, I do not see why it should be any more difficult to see the relation between the state of that imagination, the state, that is, of human sensibility in this nation, and the state of theology and religion. God is the overwhelming Reality who must be confronted and who finally will not be merely played with, or used or distorted or changed at our sweet will. He will not be changed into other gods. *Tu autem idem ipse es.* Thou art always the same. We must meet Him on the terms of what He really is and not on the terms of our own constructions and our own private dreams or of our own pure and univocal ideas. He can be covered up or uncovered, according to the habits of soul we have formed. There are no two stronger determinants of which way we shall choose than the habits and state of our conscience and the habits and state of our art.

But the reality of God, I say it reverently, is only one of the two elements in the theological picture. The other is the reality of man. I cannot put things more simply than by saying that as man must deal with God as He is (and art will help give him all the intermediate habits that will help him do so), God and the true artist must have this wonderful point of alliance that *they* both deal with the reality of man. Not with a man with two feet and the top of a head, not with an exploitable and manipulatable machine, not with a charming fool, not with a pleasant dream figure, but with man as God has made him and as the true artist continues to discover him. He is wonderfully and powerfully made for good and for bad. He has the roots of every one of the capital sins in him, and also the roots of glory. God did not make one thing called man and then, to save him, lead an altogether other thing to glory through His grace. And so with the two great habits of the real artist: he deals with the actual and concrete materials of man as he is and shall be forever; but he, too, has a kind of natural grace to confer upon these materials—he has his own forms of judgment and his own rhythmic ways of leading man through himself and the world to peace and to beauty.

Let us, therefore, never ask of the artist, out of a rootless and ill-conceived piety or sentimentality of our own, that he deal with man as he is *not*. This is not an appeal for sordid realism; it is a reminder that the artist must do in his small way what God does in His great way. This essential point, this defense of the place of human sensibility in religion and in art, will, I think, be considerably clarified by a reading of the Bible and a study of the dealings of God with the Jewish people. And may I take the liberty of recommending the reading of a few central pages in the wonderful commentary on this subject by the Benedictine scholar Dom Celestin Charlier in his *The Christian Approach to the Bible* (pp. 147–153). From these pages I take the following lines on the great figure of David:

> . . . David, the brightest jewel in humanity's crown, with something of the divine in his bearing. It is hard to know what to marvel at more in this most natural of men, his triumphs or his failures, the beauty of his love or the passion of his lust, the depths to which he fell or the heights to which his love of Yahweh led him. Men had gone before him who gave some hint of the Messiah, and others would follow him to complete the picture. Isaiah showed us the future nobility, Jeremiah the throbbing sensitiveness, Nehemiah the tranquility and the Maccabees the peace-loving and heroic generosity. But David was all of these things. In him was achieved the paradox of man made to God's image and likeness, yet clamoring for salvation from the depths of his soul. There would be none like him again until one came who took on the "likeness of sinful flesh."

It is something like this image of man which we must restore to our national culture. It is an image far, far beyond the sights of the present image-makers—save for the fine and sometimes great exceptions whom we all love and admire. It is an image which requires the collaboration of many artists and creative theologians and many other people. It will require the positive energies of many individuals and groups.

I have but one more point to make and it is a kind of

addendum. I have not at all meant to say that we ought to be committed to a tragic or univocally serious view of man. Perhaps the best way to put the matter would be as follows. Only after we are committed to an image of man that is serious and great, though difficult and complicated, can we allow ourselves to have fun with everything else—with fantasy, with dream, with nonsense, with every level of comedy, with a little stupidity, with a bit of violence here and there in our image-making, with ever so many other things.

For once we have rediscovered and re-established the real man, we will have the liberty of the sons of God and will be able to say that all these things, indeed everything a man can think of, save sin, can have their proper place in the image and the sensibility of man. It will not be a simple image.

THE PROBLEM OF CONTRARIETY
IN PLATO'S *PARMENIDES*

The following supplement contains the substance of the argument I presented for the meaning of Plato's *Parmenides* in a previous book, *An Approach to the Metaphysics of Plato Through the Parmenides*. I would like to think that the use of such a supplement has the effect of creating for the present book the same structure as the one which lies at the heart of that famous dialogue of the master of the Academy.

In the first half of the *Parmenides* Plato confronts himself with the ineluctable and palpable presence of a contrariety in the sensible and human world that had thus far gone against the grain of the oversimplifying intelligence. In the second half he constructs a logic, and a metaphysics, that makes sense of contrariety. Now men can no longer say that being is being and non-being is non-being, like is like and unlike is unlike, black is black and white is white, and that is that. Here we have one of the great beginnings of the exploration of the Western mind into our problem. Our culture has been working at that problem ever since. One thinks at once of Aristotle, Aquinas, Hegel, and the theorizing of

Samuel Taylor Coleridge on the *reconciliatio oppositorum*.

This book, therefore, also falls into two halves. In the first we have looked at seven concrete versions of the question of contrariety as it occurs in the actuality of our own national culture. In this supplement or second half I let Plato speak for himself as one of our great logicians and metaphysicians who has worked to fuse the many opposites of human life and thought.

It has been taken for granted that to grasp the nature of Platonism it is necessary to read all the dialogues and *synthesize* their spirit, that it is impossible to suggest any one dialogue that will serve the purposes of such a synthesis. But, if my reading is correct, it is possible to offer the *Parmenides* as precisely the work that will—with limitations, of course—answer such a need.

What is the first key to the meaning of the hypotheses, or second half of the *Parmenides*—for therein lies the essential puzzle?

They are nothing less than an analysis of the constitutive elements of anything that is a true *one,* or unity, in any order of being. I say "a" *one,* and immediately this point of translation is significant. We should not constantly read "the" One so that it suggests either the Neoplatonic or Parmenidean One or the Platonic Idea. Rather, the word "one" is meant to deal with unity wherever it is found, whether it be a sensible, a number, a definition, an Idea, the Parmenidean One, the Idea of the Good, or, though anachronistically, the Neoplatonic One. Whenever a true *one* is to be found, the total system of the eight hypotheses is meant to be a formal analysis of such a unity.

The arguments against the Ideas in the first half of the dialogue had indicated that the unity of the Idea has been destroyed by its dispersion into many instances or particulars. Every attempt to salvage the situation by calling the Ideas models or concepts, or by suggesting that they are present in things, results in similar dilemmas or ἀπορίαι. The One becomes many, the self-identical becomes separated from itself. Now the main task for Plato is really to stress that this "dilemma" of a one-become-many is not merely native to the relation between the Idea and its many participants or copies; it occurs *wherever* you have any kind of *one,* and occurs within the very *inner* ambit of such a *one.* Such a *one* is always a curious mixture of unity and multiplicity. But this mixture involves the very metaphysical structure of every entity and can be thoroughly rationalized—that is to say, we can locate all the senses in which a thing is one and is many, all the ways in which, despite dispersion and division, a thing remains one.

Plato, then, must be conceived as saying: before we can solve this problem of the breakdown of the unity of the Idea, we must universalize the problem. The dilemmas that issue from the existence of Ideas and particulars are only one manifestation of a question provoked not only by this relation existing between two different orders of reality but also by the relation between the elements of unity and multiplicity *within* an Idea looked at itself, *within* a sensible, *within* a number. What we must do, therefore, is to analyze the very nature of any being or any *one,* for the two are convertible. We must formulate *a philosophy of unity for any and every order, as well as for the relation between orders.* And this is precisely what we are given in the eight hypotheses. With this philosophy in hand, we should be able to return to the original difficulties of the first half of the dialogue and formulate adequate explanations for them. And this is one of the senses in which the second half is a "training."

Thus early, for the sake of structural clarity, I am proposing the following as the main propositions of a philosophy (or logic) of unity:

Hypothesis I: Here we study a *one* precisely as one and nothing else. Insofar as anything is one in any order, i.e., insofar as it has a principle of unity in it, this *one*, this principle of unity, is indivisible and without parts. As such it is a self-identity and does not enter into any equation or relationship with any of its parts or predicates, or with anything outside of it. But, though this principle exists, it is, as a pure indivisible, not knowable in the technical Platonic sense of knowledge or ἐπισήμη.

Hypothesis II: To advance to the point of such knowledge we must see that every *one* is, in actuality, a *Whole*, composed of principles of unity and multiplicity; it is a one and many, a limited and unlimited. Of the principle of unity in any such entity we can still say all we have said of it in Hypothesis I; therefore *the content of the latter remains as a permanent achievement, not as something to be cancelled out* by this second hypothesis. Of the Whole we can predicate a long series of qualities *and* their contraries. This series of contraries is dependent on the fundamental contrariety of oneness and multiplicity and is derived from them as foundation; one set of predicates derives from the oneness of an entity, their contraries from its multiplicity.

Hypothesis II A: There is a point of transition in time between any two contraries—such as being and non-being, motion and rest—that cannot be measured by time and cannot be characterized in terms of either of the two contraries or predicates involved. This we call the "instant" or the "sudden." Thus this section, as all the hypotheses, deals with a special problem or element or moment in the structure or history of a *one;* and it is only by understanding *which* problem is being discussed that we will fathom why the law of predicability is shifting in each hypothesis. For sometimes a hypothesis declares that both of two contrary predicates are applicable to a *one,* sometimes that neither of a given pair is applicable. And all eight sections keep shifting between this kind of affirmation and negation. Actually, there is always a good reason for the καί—καί of affirmation or the οὔτε—οὔτε of rejection. And the sense of the predicability or non-predicability of contraries changes with the problem involved, as we shall see. For example, non-predicability is the law both in respect to the "instant" of II A and the indeterminate or infinite element of IV, but the reasons behind the two negations are as different as the two phenomena under investigation in those sections.

Hypothesis III: Here begins the analysis of the nature (and structural contribution to the Whole) of the two elements in any entity: one and many, limit and unlimited. The *one* is the dominant principle, source of the unity of a Whole, and contributor to its parts of all the specificity and definiteness they may come to possess. In any entity there is only one *One* and but a single source of predicability. If the Others, or members of the Whole, receive all the predicates of contrariety that the Whole itself has received (in II), it is not that they are, *of themselves,* separate, identifiable units, but rather that they participate in the specificity of the one, i.e., through association with the principle of oneness in a thing.

Hypothesis IV: We analyze the nature of the Others (the many member parts, or unlimited, in any entity). They are, *of themselves,* an infinitely divisible multiplicity, which can be characterized by the specificity and unity of neither of any given pair of contraries.

Hypothesis V: A *one* is itself limited in relation to the rest of the real, i.e., in relation to all other *ones.* This is true because of the presence in it of *otherness* or *difference,* a form of relative non-being that limits a *one* and differentiates it from all others. Thus any *one* is a compound of being and non-being, and this contrariety is the foundation for ascribing to it a whole series of other contraries.

Hypothesis VI: As the preceding hypothesis was a study of the relative non-being of a *one* and of the type of predication that results from such a fusion of being and non-being, so this section is an analysis of what is meant by the absolute non-being of an entity and what follows for it in the way of predication. Once again, but for a different reason, neither of any two contraries can characterize it.

Hypothesis VII: So far, we have been submitting any *one* to a careful metaphysical analysis. Now suppose that the non-philosophical or "doxastic" mind analyzes the structure of a being. Such a mind does not grasp the total unity in an entity, but it attempts to keep hold of all the separate units that compose the Whole. This is impossible because this specificity of parts proceeds from the principle of total unity. We are therefore engaged in a compromising mode of thought, where the oneness of a thing and the specificity of its parts both exist and do not exist. The result is the typical confusion of being and non-being, and of all the other contraries, that is typical of what Plato calls δόξα. This hypothesis, therefore, is a study of δόξα and its approach to a *one.*

Hypothesis VIII: Once again suppose that the principle of unity does not exist at all in a *one,* and ask what are the con-

sequences for its parts (i.e., the unlimited). Neither, then,
will *these* exist. Thus it follows that the oneness in a thing,
its principle of unity, is the source not only of the predicability and specificity of its member parts (III) but also
of their very being. In other words, the unlimited makes a
contribution to the structure of an entity, but this very contribution is made possible by oneness or unity. It is only the
imagination that will conceive the ἄπειρον or unlimited as an
altogether separate and previously existing reality that
awaits the gift of specificity and form from oneness.

A skeleton outline of the dramatic movement of the first
half of the dialogue might be put thus:

I. ZENO

Zeno is the proposer of a set of antinomies that exist in the
sensible order. He finds that, if we accept any kind of principle of multiplicity in being, *then certain oppositions or
contrarieties will exist in the same sensible entity;* the like
will also be unlike; the one will also be a multiplicity. But
this, he says, is absurd.

In a sense, the logic of the *Parmenides* will be forced to return at least partially to the original ground of Zeno and try
courageously to face a possibility that it consistently rejects
until the very beginning of its second half (i.e., until the
eight hypotheses). It is a good beginning to say that the contrarieties of the sensible order cannot be solved by remaining within that order and that we must have a theory of Ideas.
But the logic of things will finally force us to acknowledge
that even in the Ideas, indeed in the whole range of being,
what is one is itself many, what is like is itself unlike. That is
to say, it will be seen that contrariety can and must exist

within the same entity, whether the latter be a sensible, an Idea, or anything else.

I do not think, therefore, that we really understand either the weakness or the force of Zeno's arguments or the drama of the dialogue unless we see that Zeno turns out to be half right. His partial function is to initiate the great debate by stating the problem of the one-many, the problem of contrariety, in that primitive way in which it strikes the senses of the ordinary man who sees that sensible realities are a curious mélange of ἀπορίαι. The whole first half is the story of the twisting and turning of Socrates in order to escape the confusion of these dilemmas, to keep the *one* a pure one, and the many a pure, isolated many, devoid of all oneness. He makes three attempts to do this: through the theory of Ideas as a theory (1) of participation, (2) of imitation, and (3) of conceptualism. None of these, as stated in the first half of the dialogue, succeeds in maintaining the unity and purity of the Idea. He therefore finally abandons the very effort to preserve these qualities. He is compelled (in the eight hypotheses) to work out an interior logic of all being, according to which any *one* (sensible, Idea, definition, number, etc.) is a mixture of one-many, like-unlike, etc.

Thus, a simple dramatic plan. Zeno is largely right. Contrariety exists within the same field of being, within the same entity. The crude and primitive perception of contrariety is correct. But at the end of the hypothesis, we shall have a system of logic that will have completely *rationalized,* made logical, this kind of "dilemma" of contraries. What was a fact but logically impossible will have become logically possible and understandable. The primitive view will have been refined to the point of philosophical intelligibility.

This, I take it, is the dramatic status of the first steps in the dialogue, the argument of Zeno.

II. SOCRATES

The Ideas, Proposed as Solution of Contrariety

This seems to Socrates to be the all-important necessity of the moment: to discover a region of being where the contraries are, as it were, sorted out with absolute purity, for it is thus that we are presumptuous enough, at this stage, to think that Zeno will be answered. What is more simple to say than that a thing is one by participating in oneness, and many by participating in multiplicity? The two realities that are participated in are completely diverse and thus the irritating question of contrariety seems to be resolved.

About this kind of resolution two things may be said: (1) It is a relatively crude form of the theory of Ideas and tries by a sort of sleight of hand to answer the dilemmas proposed. Even if it were true—which is not altogether the case—that qualities can be isolated in terms of the world of pure being, of the Ideas, this would not quite remove the difficulty that they still co-exist in the form of contrary pairs in sensibles. It would still remain true that, even though there be a region where oneness is not multiplicity, the sensible *one* is also a many. In a word, we would have constructed a world which would have somewhat answered the exigencies of human speech and thought, which *does* isolate a pure self-identity for each quality. But we would not at all have solved the confusing testimony of the sense world, where qualities are still strangely intermingled. The world of language and thought would have been given fairly satisfactory objects, but the world of logic would still have failed to confront the order of the senses. We would still be no better off than we were after concluding a reading of the Poem of Parmenides itself.

(2) I am also going to propose that the theory of participation given so far is early and thoroughly unsatisfactory for the purposes of the present emergency. Before the dialogue is

completed, it will be replaced by a much more subtle form of participation—indeed, by a form that is revolutionary to Platonic thought.

The final and refined theory of participation in the eight hypotheses can be summarized roughly in the following diagram:

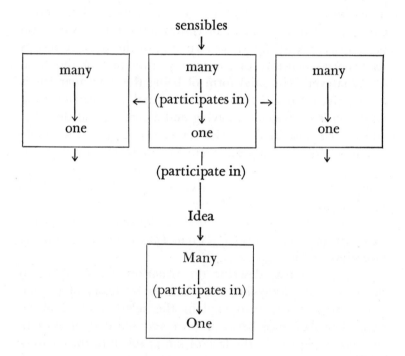

Here we have the expression of a whole series of participations: (1) *Within* the sensible and *within* the Idea, the many elements of any one thing participate in, share, "have" their being from the principle of oneness or unity in any such sensible or Idea. There is only one reality that truly *is* in either sensible or Idea; that is its principle of unity; all its multiple elements *have,* and derive from, this indivisible being. Thus participation becomes a law internal to every level of being. According to this law, the principle of unity in an entity exists absolutely, that of multiplicity receives only a relative being; thus the phenomenon of contrariety is severely modified, for we no longer have two *absolute* contraries opposed to each other. This point is critically important. (2) Thus internally structured (in such a way as will *inwardly* explicate its own problem of contrariety), the sensible also participates *essentially* in the structure of the Idea. It derives its essential structure of contrariety from that of the Idea. (3) Whatever existential form of being the particular has is also derived from the Idea. This actual but participating existence is once again a having and a sharing and does not add to the idea in any strict sense. (4) Finally, the whole system of Idea-and-all-its-particulars is a One-many that can avoid the impossibilities of contrariety through the same distinction of absolute and relative forms of being. There is never a real duality of principles in any such "organism." It is, then, simply not correct to view the one and the many as *a pair of contrary principles that have equal status* on the same level of being.

Perhaps we may describe the situation that is about to develop in the following way. The early theory of participation was sufficient to explain the relation of absolute-dependent existence between Idea and sensible; it is completely inadequate in the face of the problem of the compossibility of contraries.

III. THE OBJECTIONS OF PARMENIDES

Plato allows the present arguments to take their course unanswered; he will in due time add many other less easily

manageable antinomies that exist at and in every level of
being; in this way he will have forced himself to construct
a general logic of a one-that-is-always-many; thus equipped
with a more refined instrument, he will be able to deal with
all the antinomies that seem to proceed from the relation of
any *one* to its many, whether the one in question be an Idea,
a sensible, a number, a definition (enclosing multiple elements in its very inward and essential structure), or a transcendent *one* or Idea (relating itself to a multiple class of
particulars). What he needs is a general metaphysics of any
one-many able to demonstrate that, no matter what the internal division in a *one,* it remains an absolute indivisible
and, no matter what the external dispersion of a one in its
particulars, it again remains indivisible and unmultiplied.
Once again, therefore, I say that Plato allows the present
dialectic to take its course; for by its insertion of disunity
and dispersion into the Idea it is at least forcing the discussion in a right and necessary direction.

HYPOTHESIS I

Briefly, the whole section tells us that, wherever there is a
one, certain basic things may already be said about it. It is,
in the first place, a pure indivisible without parts, without
any structural division of beginning, middle, or end. Already
it is difficult to see how such a first logic does not immediately collapse for sensibles, but that question will have to be
discussed in its separate place. We are further told that this
one is not identical with any real or hypothetical part or
member of itself. Therefore, all predication is impossible for
it. And this is true not only of a Neoplatonic One but of
anything that is truly one, even of a sensible. Since it is
rigorously a self-identity, we should not even say that it is

the same as itself; for, as Aristotle himself points out, even the motion of sameness with self connotes a duality. But the principle of oneness, precisely as oneness, precludes *all* duality. Whether we take all the negations with which Parmenides describes his One or all those with which the Neoplatonists will describe theirs, the really interesting thing to note is that Plato is referring the same series of negations to all unity. One or two of the isolated exceptions that Plato refuses to adopt from the predicates of either Parmenides or the Neoplatonists (granted always the anarchronism) are analyzed below.

Thus, in brief, the first hypothesis lays down the two basic laws of non-divisibility and non-predicability for anything that is truly a *one*. Certainly it will be necessary to discover other structural principles and laws existing in a *one,* but these will be the business of subsequent hypotheses and will in no sense cancel the achievement of the first.

EXPLANATION OF SHIFTING PREDICATION

One ought not to decide beforehand that Plato is playing with words and performing anti-rational tricks to show that, if you are clever enough, all things can be demonstrated to be true and not true of the same thing. Historically, what Plato was confronted with was an over-simple understanding of the principle of contradiction. According to this simplification, there is an absolute dichotomy between being and non-being—if a thing is, it can in no sense not be; if it is one of two contraries, it can in no sense be the other. It was therefore necessary to supply a training that would indicate to the mind all the refinements this dichotomy was neglecting. Far from being scandalized at the constant manner in which Plato, through the course of the *Parmenides,* will be shattering this overly incisive dichotomy, we must first learn to ask what principle in a *one,* or what quality in it, or what phenomenon in which it is engaged, is being brought into question. Isolate the problem and you have your hands on the root reason in each case for the rejection or affirmation of *both* contraries, of both being and non-being and all other pairs.

THE CONCLUDING LINES OF HYPOTHESIS I

The facile thing at this point would be to yield to the obvious strength of these contrasting tests and to acknowledge what seems quite clear: that at the end of Hypothesis I Plato has an unnamable monster on his hands in the shape of a pure and indivisible *one* that cannot even exist. Apart from the Neoplatonists, I believe this is a universal conclusion.

The major difficulty here is that these lines have been isolated and have not been studied in the light of the whole dialogue. More important still, they have not been examined in the light of the habits of expression that characterize the whole Platonic corpus.

The first part of the dialogue had ended with the insistence, against every assault, that there must be Ideas and that the whole possibility of human language and philosophy depends upon them. In entire consonance with this position, the first hypothesis has opened the dialectical defense of the Ideas by asserting the existence of absolutely unique, separate factors that can in no way be confused one with the other. Whether these separate factors are found in the pure form in the transcendent Ideas, or in the shape of human definitions of the same, or in the participating mode of visible objects, we can apply to them practically all the qualities or negations of the Parmenidean or Neoplatonic One. There is an element in everything truly a "thing" that is simple and undivided. So true is this that such an element will not share the divisibilities of space and time. Such indivisible factors can and must exist. Therefore the first hypothesis rightly begins with such a doctrine.

But it is entirely another thing to say that these factors can be known as such, known in their sheer indivisibility and simplicity. A *one,* precisely as one, is not "known" as such by the rational mind, which, we shall see, always knows in terms of the one and multiple. *De facto,* there can be and there is real knowledge of things—and that in the highest Platonic sense of the word. But this is only possible because there are in things more than absolutely unifying factors. The existence of the latter has been asserted by common sense and philosophical intuition in the first half of the dialogue. Thereafter, in the first hypothesis, elaborate dialectic has added to this assertion the most exhaustive description of the simple Ideas that is to be found so far in the dialogues. But it will be the business of the second hypothesis to discover those further principles in essences that bring them into the range of human knowledge. Our paradox, however, will remain: that, no matter what the multiplicity now entering the picture, the pure One survives it all.

HYPOTHESIS II

The simplest way of describing the logical advance of the second over the first hypothesis is to say that oneness now emerges, no longer as a pure indivisible, but as a whole of parts. "Parts" is the Platonic word, though perhaps "members" or "factors" would better serve our purpose and would be less suggestive of a restriction of our logic to sensible parts. Never for a moment does the dialogue abandon the principle that there is an indivisible of pure oneness in every entity of every order, but we now learn that every such *one* also contains a multiplicity of some kind, whether sensible, numerical, conceptual, or transcendent. Throughout this hypothesis and all those that follow (with the possible exception of the fifth), this multiple element of many factors will be described by the name of the "others" or "other."

It is also possible to say that the subject of the second hypothesis is that of communion, or κοινωνία. But this actually is the same as saying that a *one* is a whole. Up to now, our first metaphysical analysis of any unity has revealed it as an isolated entity that is without division and that of itself enters into no relation with any other entity inside or outside of it. Now we become aware that a number of such units can coalesce to form a large unit, and this will serve as our first rough description of what κοινωνία means: the ability of any two or more factors so to relate themselves that coexistence in a whole is possible. This is by no means all that Plato will have to say about the nature of communion or relation. Indeed, as we shall see, all the succeeding hypotheses, save the fifth, can very well be understood as serving the function of refining the Platonic notion of κοινωνία, or the coexistence of things.

In brief, Hypothesis II comes to the following general conclusions: (1) any one thing is really a complexus of elements or parts and these constitute a whole, one element of which is indivisible, the other divisible (a one-many); (2) further exploration reveals that the parts to be discovered in a *one* are infinite; in reality, then, the constituting elements of a *one* are the limit and the unlimited; this is a fundamental contrariety rooted in all being and is the source for the ascription of all other contraries to any unity; (3) from this fundamental contrariety proceed a number of others: in itself— in another; moving—at rest; same—different; like—unlike; equal—unequal; (4) the two basic elements of one-many, indivisible-divisible, limit-unlimited, are then put to special use in solving the antinomies of the spatial and temporal continua. Thus the hypothesis goes further than being a study of the possibility of the coexistence of factors within unified wholes; it will, for example, be but a minor part of its work to show that there is such a communion between oneness and being. Its more difficult task is to establish the κοινωνία of *contrary* elements in all being, and in this it begins to fulfill the implicit promises made in the first half of the dialogue. At the same time, the hypothesis must not be conceived as going further than it actually does. It is quite satisfied to establish the *co-presence* of contraries in a *one* and to leave to succeeding sections the more subtle explication of the metaphysical *relations between* such elements as the one and many or the limit and unlimited. For example, we shall have later occasion to see that it is not quite true to say that there is in any *one* a one *and* a many, a limited *and* an unlimited. In Hypothesis III and VIII, the one, or principle of unity, will emerge as the exclusive source both of predication and existence for its members, and will thus avoid being confronted with a *strict* division or multiplicity of elements in being. I indicate so much at this point only to stress once again the fundamental reliance of Plato on the Eleatic logic. Here, in the second hypothesis, that system is being corrected to allow for multiple elements in every order of reality.

The very initial description of this One-Whole already creates a basic antinomy in every entity: each *one* is a whole (which we know to be an absolute indivisible) and each is a many. In a word, two factors are in communion because they exist within the common ambit of some total unity. And this breakdown into antinomical elements is true of any *one,* whether a sensible or a number or a definition or an Idea. As a consequence we are already in the presence of a phenomenon that Socrates has said will fill him with wonder if it were true. He has said that it is easy enough to solve the co-presence of contraries, if such a problem is found only on the level of sensibles; for a sensible particular might participate in the Idea of unity and also in the Idea of plurality and thus, without difficulty, be both one and many. This now turns out to be a superficial solution; for clearly enough, and still from the very analysis of the concept of oneness, the very Idea of oneness, and every Idea (they are all *ones*), is, upon further analysis, a composite of contraries, of one and many.

This would seem, on the face of things, only to intensify the difficulty. Have we done any more than universalize the dilemma? It will be Hypothesis III that will shortly have to bend itself to solving the problem of how a *one* can be many and still remain *one* in the strictest sense. But, fortunately, there are senses in which this very universalizing process will be the means of dissolving important difficulties raised against participation. For example, it is true that an indivisible Idea, when it is participated in by such divided phenomena as a man or a beast, becomes dispersed through the parts of these. But if we show that, no matter how many the parts into which *any* entity in *any* order is dispersed, it need not lose the quality of oneness or indivisibility, where is there any sting in the eristic of such objections? Indeed, if the reader is ever on the alert to learn from this γυμνασία of the eight hypotheses, he will be picking up all those clues that will enable him to answer the difficulties of the first part of the dialogue; he will also be better able to cope with the whole Aristotelian critique of the Ideas, and he will be ready to handle the attack from the original unpurified Eleatic logic. He will not even be frightened by such an objection as this, that if the transcendent Idea is present in many particulars, it becomes distinct and separated from itself; for he will have learned to search into the sense in which, despite this multiplying and separating presence of an Idea in many sensibles, it remains uniquely one and unseparated from itself. But he will no longer solve such questions after the Eleatic manner by denying the evidence of the senses or refusing to face the facts; rather, he will be equipped both to "save the phenomena" and to save the substantial elements of the Eleatic logic.

The study of the next set of contrary predicates (likeness-unlikeness) will contain sense only if we return to the memory of the original difficulties presented to us by Parmenides in the first half of the dialogue. For example: there we had been told that if a transcendent Idea finds itself present in some way or other in many concrete instances, it is then divided from itself and loses its original unity and purity. True enough, Plato would seem to be saying here in the second half, but we must learn to distinguish a sense in which it is so divided and a sense in which, despite this multiplication, it remains undivided from itself. And so with other problems involving division and dispersion of unities. There will be a mode of existence for any unified fact according to which, despite all division, it remains an absolute indivisible; another according to which it suffers dispersion and manyness. We cannot be trained too carefully in making these distinctions and in understanding these "dilemmas" and their possible solution. The present texts are nothing but somewhat exaggerated examples of this kind of training.

HYPOTHESIS II A

It should now be clear that it is the intention of the eight hypotheses to discuss as many problems in the logic, the metaphysics, and the physics of the Platonic system as is possible in their brief compass. The over-all question that receives most attention, at least on the dramatic surface of the second half of the dialogue, is that of the predication of contraries. And the laws of this predication, we have said, shift according to the nature of the phenomenon being studied. We have discovered why it was impossible to ascribe either of two contraries to the phenomenon of unity as such in the opening hypothesis. We have, in the second, likewise discovered the validity of the application of both contraries to the general phenomenon of a whole which is a one-many and to all the subordinate phenomena discussed within such a new world. Now, in the appendix that is added to this section (it is traditionally called II A), the external form of predication suddenly and briefly returns to the original form of the first hypothesis: that is to say, we again deny that either of two contraries can be applied to a *one*. But we have by this time acquired the dialectical habit of being on guard for the emergence of a new question that will call for a new logic of predicates. This appendix, then, does not in any way cancel out any previous series of propositions. It simply recognizes that it has left something undiscussed and proceeds to discuss it. What, therefore, is the new subject?

It is the nature of the *interval,* or *point of transition,* that separates two contraries in the time process of passage from one to the other.

In a word, we are here examining all the types of becoming, under the form of the passage of one opposite to another. These opposites include the following: all coming-to-be, or passage from non-being to being; all "passing-away," or passage from being to non-being; all coming-to-be-one (combination) and coming-to-be-many (separation); all change in quality (alteration) and quantity (increase and decrease); all passage from rest to motion and motion to rest (locomotion).

We may reason that the very nature of becoming and time

involves some kind of entity not measurable in terms of being, some point of time not measurable in terms of time, at which it is impossible to predicate of a changing thing either one of two involved contraries. There is no calculable transition between being and non-being, for there is nothing between them. Parmenides himself had said that there is being that is and non-being that is not and there is nothing between this dichotomy. Plato's method of handling the dichotomy is far more subtle; for this *instant* is only the most recent in a series of "intervals" that he has discovered between being and non-being; they exist, each one of them, but cannot be expressed in terms of the positive being of Hypothesis I. Change is indeed real, but it cannot be explained in terms of such a positive real as that of the first hypothesis. It is, however, explained in terms of a positive form of non-being.

HYPOTHESIS III

It is true that every cosmic factor is distinct and self-identical—but it is also related in a negative or positive way with every other such factor. It can either fuse or not fuse with every other being. Now, if between any two concepts there is such a positive relationship, then there is a weaving together, a συμπλοκή. If in any way they are compatible, they participate one in the other (μετέχειν). There is between them a communion, a κοινωνία. But this relatedness and these terms do not actually introduce a difficulty distinct from our earlier one. For all such terms either mean that things that are thus fused are really being described as things that can exist together within the same individual; or they fall under some relation—which relation may be considered as a higher, unifying fact containing such members. Again the question,

If these self-identical facts are true units, is there—can there be—a true unity which embraces them? If so, how shall we describe it?

There is no form of the definite that is not in the *one*, that is not the *one*. It pervades all and determines all. This is true if we look first at the unity of all the parts as a whole. How now does this unity differ from the *one*? How, that is to say, does the sum of the parts differ from the *one*? This whole of parts *has*, participates in, the unity that the *one is* —and whatever unity is had by this totality is a derivative of the *one*. Of themselves all the parts are a sheer many— indeed, not even this, for a true many is a multitude of units, whereas this is a pure infinite.

These parts, into which a part may itself definitively and finitely be broken down, have their derivation and their definiteness from the *One*. Indeed, if this process of division is not in actuality endless, if, for example (at the end of the process of diaeresis), we come to an indivisible, an ἄτομον, that cannot be dichotomized, this giving of a pause and a term to the infinite has the same source. But so too with all the inner regions of the division of any concept. At any stage of diaeresis we have the possibility of the infinite division of a genus into its subordinate species, thus:

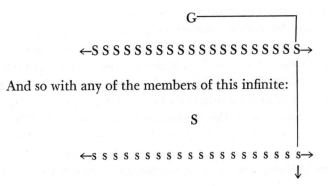

And so with any of the members of this infinite:

But the vertical line that is accumulating the elements of the final definition is exceedingly definite and is giving pause to the infinite at every stage of the process. This is due to the constant limiting function of the *one* and *cannot possibly be explained by the power for choice or determination held by each superior genus in the species.* For this power is of itself infinite and unlimited, and therefore no power at all.

HYPOTHESIS IV

If the *one* were not in nature different from the unlimited, if one were not separated from the other in the sense of being different, then (1) the unlimited would also be one, (2) everything in an entity would be an unqualified unit, (3) we would be back in a world of entities with a completely discrete structure of separate units that have no unity among them, and (4) the whole sense world, with its varieties of one-manys occurring in the phenomena of space and time, would be impossible.

There is, in fact, only one statement being repeated again and again through the fourth hypothesis: only the one, or principle of unity in a thing, is one; the others, or members of that unity, are of themselves in no sense one (though oneness may be communicated to them). And this holds true even in the fully structured and determined entity where there is no "separation" and the process of communication and participation may be called complete. Even in that moment the unlimited others still contribute no determination.

We can deny all the contraries in such a "reality" as this Platonic indeterminate—first of all, the fundamental contrariety of a one-many. For if the "others," or the principle of multiplicity, are not one, neither are they a "many," which is nothing save a numerable set of *units*. Further, since there is no quality of determined unity in them they cannot be like, for that would be to possess *one* quality; nor like and unlike, for that would be to have two *unit* qualities. And for the same reason we may say the same thing of all the contrary pairs, whether same-different, or motion-rest, or coming and ceasing to be. They will never be found in the indeterminate.

We could hardly be told more clearly that in any reality or in any order there is only one *one*, and this alone specifies a thing to be what it is, both in its unity and in its multiple aspects. It is this proposition that may be considered the combined achievement of Hypotheses III and IV. And it is not again necessary to indicate at any length how the achievement flows from, and corresponds so much with, the Parmenidean logic. We may finally note that, after the dissection of a *one* that occurs in Hypothesis II, we have in an important sense restored the original unity of an entity as we saw it in the opening hypothesis. *Thus, in the first half of the hypotheses of the dialogue there is a sort of cyclical movement that is now completed.*

HYPOTHESIS V

Plato proceeds in these pages to the bold conclusion that every factor thinkable by the human mind is a mixture of being and non-being, same and other, absolute and relative. In brief, Hypothesis V is an anticipation of some of the principal conclusions of the *Sophist* on the relation of being to non-being.

Plato is the first to insert non-being into the heart of being without identifying the two. True enough, the pages of a dialogue like the *Republic* are replete with the description of a midway entity that is a combination of being and non-being, but these texts deal exclusively with the structure of the world of becoming. The merit of the *Parmenides* is that, as it has promised, it transfers this interior relation to an order of concepts that will hold for all things. Thus far in the dialogue we have dealt with such contraries, as One and Many, Like and Unlike, Equal and Unequal, and have seen that, as the specific problem varies, neither or both of these contraries within any one set can be applied to a *one*. It is the business of Hypothesis V to examine the profoundest of all the pairs of opposites and to indicate that both being and non-being can be predicated of any one thing.

The very foundation of any Other thing is the interior structure of a *one*, that mixture of being and non-being that prevents it from exhausting the whole range of oneness and thus makes multiplicity possible. It is, therefore, purely a relation between *ones* and is a sort of interval separating them. As such it takes the place of the κενόν, or void, of the Atomists. And it is quite clear that, instead of the external mechanical relation between being and the void, we have on our hands a far more subtle attempt to introduce non-being into the very fibre of being and thus to mediate our original severe dichotomy.

Actually, what we have just seen is the first serious attempt to describe a non-being that is relational (we remember Aristotle's use of the words *logical* and *accidental*). It would perhaps be too much to begin to attach the final system of principles of Aristotle to these findings, but the fact remains that we are here faced with a milestone in the history of Greek philosophy. It is not too much to say that the formation of this concept of relational non-being created a new ontology and logic within which the mind of Aristotle could operate.

HYPOTHESES VI AND VIII

Now that Plato has untied one of the Gordian knots of pre-Socratic philosophy by this exposition of the existence and nature of relative non-being, he can afford to be completely free and uninhibited in the description of the absolute non-being of a *one* that follows. The classical distinction between the two forms of nothingness having been made, it is now possible to repeat and to accept—at times in almost literal fashion—everything that Parmenides has said of pure nothingness. And this is exactly the function of Hypothesis VI.

For Plato's complete doctrine of absolute non-being we should have to examine the joint contributions of this and the final hypothesis of the dialogue. For the two stand close to each other in a tightly knit fashion. First of all, in the sixth, if a *one* is not (i.e., if there is simply no principle of unity in an entity), what can be said of this *one?* Nothing. It exists in no way, has no relation to being, cannot be described by either of any two contraries, and cannot be the object of thought. This in sum is the message of the sixth hypothesis. The final hypothesis goes much further: it announces that if there is not such a principle as a *one* then neither does the principle of manyness or the infinite or the "others" exist. There is literally and absolutely nothing.

HYPOTHESIS VII

Essentially some inferior kind of thinking is the manner of all δόξα. According to its most steadfast meaning in the dialogues, it is a faculty midway between knowledge and ignorance and, consistently with the Platonic habit of defining a faculty by its object, the object of *doxa* is the mixture of being and non-being that is the status of becoming. In accordance with the very nature of its object, its conclusions are never fixed; its virtue and goodness are inferior; its courage is without wisdom; its poetic insights are highly limited; its political insights are based on shifting opportunism; and its most accurate physical discoveries can never have the exactitude of true knowledge.

But the δόξα of which there is now question is more widely ranging than any of these concepts. For the *one* that we are analyzing through all the hypotheses is the notion of oneness as such and is representative of unity in any order. But the concepts of δόξα that we have just enumerated restrict themselves to the order of becoming and to the obscurities that essentially reside in it. Now we deal with a δόξα (with all its limitations and imprecisions) that can invade any order of things, whether that of becoming or that of the Ideas. There is a type of imprecision of which even those who believe in the Idea can be guilty. Thus we are told in the *Sophist* that only he who accurately divides the kinds is the true philosopher; but, even more importantly, we are warned in the *Philebus* that we must not go too quickly from the indeterminate to the final, completely differentiated *one*. If we do, the sense is, kind will merge into kind and the result will be considerable obscurity of definition. The *one* will not have been allowed to produce a definite number of factors, and we shall be left with an impression of any one entity that is similar to the very general description of the vague impression of "seeming" Plato is about to give us in detail.

If we had been consistent according to the consistency of the Eleatic logic, either we would have seen any one thing as a thoroughly homogeneous entity (only being or sheer unity would remain); or if we had cancelled such a One, then we would have been faced with nothing but absolute non-being. If, on the other hand, we had chosen the Platonic logic, it would have been dealing with a world of *ones* that are thoroughly unified *and* thoroughly articulated. However, δόξα has attempted to keep this articulation and otherness without unity. The consequence should have been a completely indeterminate being without any definite factors. Actually, the result of its curious compromise is a confusion of the contraries. And for the first time in the dialogue we have come across an illegitimate and impossible predication of contrary pairs.

CONCLUSION

Very early in this study I suggested that one of the severest problems with which Plato had to deal was the complete dichotomy between being and non-being that had been created by the Parmenidean logic. Let us now consider for a moment how this more sensitively conceived theory of participation has attacked and resolved some of the dilemmas inherent in such a dichotomy.

Participation is a concept that succeeds in locating a world midway between being and non-being. And every metaphysics must locate such a region if it is to have any success in resolving such problems as motion and change in the sensible, and the phenomenon of unity in any complex being in any order. Because Aristotle was particularly interested in the problem of the logical possibility of *becoming,* of various forms of non-being coming into being, he too was forced to find an answer to the Eleatic propositions that would have made such a transition impossible. This he does by his theory of potential being, and much of his metaphysics is an explanation of the qualities of *being and non-being* that are resident in the related Ideas of potency, privation, matter and genus. All these notions are attempts to mediate the type of logic that would insist that either a thing is or it is not; and if it already is it cannot come to be, if it is not, again it cannot come to be. If, therefore, there is such a thing as new being in the world, it had in some fashion not to be before its appearance, and must by equal necessity have already been in existence in some fashion. Both these things can be said of potency. But where Aristotle solved dilemmas by his concept of matter and potency, Plato did so by his theory of participation. First of all he thus resolved the ἀπορία of unity.

Unfortunately, it has not been clear that the problem of unity in any composed being involved the same Eleatic structural dilemma. If one is to establish the possibility of real unity or oneness in a complex Idea or sensible or definition or number, it is once again necessary to mediate the dichotomy of Parmenides. For if all the elements of any entity in any order exist on an equal basis so far as their status of being is concerned, if all things in this entity *are* in an "absolute" manner, then they are all in a very real sense absolute units and it is impossible to create anything but the most artificial kind of unity between such members of a Whole. Superficially at least, the unelaborated theory of Ideas seemed to have left itself open to such criticism, and a good deal of the critique of Aristotle is based on such impossibilities *on the level of unity*.

Now the metaphysics of Plato was especially concerned with this ἀπορία of unity, and we must understand how it is resolved by his theory of participation. A brief review of the sketch of the structure of the separate orders of the real as given above will indicate that in each entity in each order there is only *one being*. By his total elimination of non-being, Parmenides had ended by using the concept of One Being on a cosmic scale only. Plato is far more adroit in employing the concept, and in his metaphysics we find it present in every *thing* that is. Everything else in an entity—all its member concepts, or its compositional matter, or its structural parts— exists only by the mode of participation in the "absolute" being or unity of the thing—which dominates, determines, and produces the "parts." These, therefore, exist in a midway status between being and non-being. It is impossible to say, in an over-simplification, that they *are*. But it is equally impossible to describe them in terms of absolute non-being (as in the description of Hypothesis VI). Thus, in the case of the sensible, if I may use an example that will serve a double purpose, there is a double type of midway region that mediates the original dichotomy. Within the organism of the sensible, its parts only participate in the being of its *one*. It is not to be said, over-simply, that they are or are not. And thus we avoid the need of treating them as absolute units from which true unity could never be compounded. For the general dictum of Aristotle would remain true that two things can only become one if they were never two in the first place. But within the larger organism of the Idea- sensibles, the total organism of a sensible, including its ab- solute principle of being, must be considered as existing according to the mode of participation. It only *shares* in the being of the Idea and it is wrong to consider it a totally new entity which can ever disturb or disperse the original unity of the Idea. There *is* only one absolute in any particular class of entities, and that is the Idea. So far as sensibles are con- cerned, the whole Platonic description of the midway world of δόξα must take over, as a mediating world between being and non-being. If we now re-assess the nature of δόξα in terms of an explanation based on the participation theory of our dialogue, we will be able to use such a midway kind of thinking everywhere in such a way as everywhere to solve the problem of oneness.

Otherness

There are three other modes of being-non-being in the logic of Plato—and therefore three other ways of breaking the Eleatic dichotomy. These are the concepts of Otherness, of relation, and of the "instant." They are all types of mediation between being and non-being, and there is some valid sense in which all may be said to be further types of the idea of participation. They "have" their being only in relation to some absolute form of being.

Unity, after all, is but one Platonic problem. Otherness, or difference, is an equally compelling phenomenon that demands an explanation and the development of some kind of theory of "logical possibility." And here again we begin to see in how many subtle ways Plato has modified the original concept of absolute being. If once more we take the example of a sensible, we have seen that it contains an "absolute" principle of being and unity. It also contains an indeterminate set of factors that we call the infinite and that is a combination of being and non-being. But such a sensible *one* is the only one *one,* whereas an evidential world fills us with impressions of many other realities. The sensible entity we are considering must, then, in a still further sense, be a compound of both being and non-being. For it both *is* itself and *is not* all the other things that are not itself. To resolve this phenomenon of limitation, it is necessary to realize that each *one* is constructed of an absolute phase of being (by which it is itself according to a mode of full positivity) and a negative phase of non-being that is a negation of identity with anything else. This latter we call Otherness, or difference, and it is immaterial whether we call it relative being or relative non-being. At any rate it only exists by a participation in the positive being of the *one* that it limits or negates. Once again, it cannot possibly be described as absolute non-being, for in that eventuality there would be no such thing as difference and we would be reduced once more to the perfect world-homogeneity of the Eleatics.

Relation

No world view would be nearly adequate if it restricted itself to an explanation of the phenomenon of limitation and negation in all the *ones* of the world. It would simply have established a logic of difference or of negative relations between things. It would not at all have accounted for the endless series of positive relations that hold between *ones* and that bind the universe together in larger unities of explanation. Therefore, since up to the moment we have limited ourselves to the formulation of a relative type of non-being (which exists only by its relation to the full positivity of a *one* and which explains the problem of negative relationship), we must now turn to the construction of a form of non-being that is not only relative but also positive in its bearing. And thus we shall have to be able to say three things of this new reality: of itself, it *is not,* for only the positive *ones are* in any absolute sense; but secondly, it *is* in a relative sense (relative to those *ones* it ties together in some bond of explanation); it participates in their being. Thirdly, this relativity is positive in its nature, for the relations in question are positive and no longer merely negative and differentiating. And as a result of all this we are slowly amassing a series of forms of participating being, all of which differ among

themselves by virtue of the different problems they are meant
to resolve.

The "Instant"

Finally, we must not suppose that Plato was uninterested in
all the evidence of motion and change that the external
world communicates to us. But, as in every previous case, the
inevitable ἀπορία of the Eleatic dichotomy between being and
non-being intervenes to make the problem difficult in the
order of logic, if not in the order of actuality. Plato's explanation is not the explanation of Aristotle, but it en-
counters the same problem and the same necessity of finding
an intermediary reality. There *is* such a thing as change,
there *is* an actual moment of transition between A and B.
And yet this is a moment that can be said *not to be,* for at
this point a one is the full positivity of neither A nor B.
It is in process between the two. We will call this mysterious
moment the "instant" and will realize that it is a compound
of being and non-being. Yet, if we are perfectly to grasp the
nature of this entity, we must go further by insisting that it
is impossible to predicate either being or non-being of it. For
all change is a passage from being to non-being, or the reverse, and the point of passage must be neither of these.

Here we get a fairly accurate picture of the sense in which
Plato is always pairing contraries throughout the dialogue.
The different contraries are meant to be a descriptive explanation of the different characteristics of any entity under discussion. Here we are discussing the moment of transition in
change, and the sum of the four contraries will serve together
as a complete descriptive definition of this moment. There is
a sense in which the "instant" is and is not, neither is nor is
not, and the sum total of these senses is the limit to which

we can go in our explanation of the "instant." This kind of *summarizing* definition of our moment of transition in motion or change can serve as an effective analogy of the nature of all eight hypotheses of the *Parmenides*. If we collect the conclusions of all eight, if we have now seized as one system all the uses of contrary predicates in all the hypotheses, we will have the most accurate possible definition, in Platonic terms, of what a *one* is.

This total series of affirmations and rejections of contrariety is, as I interpret, the Platonic definition of a *one*.